Giuseppe Frassinetti

A dogmatic catechism

From the Italian of Frassinetti

Giuseppe Frassinetti

A dogmatic catechism
From the Italian of Frassinetti

ISBN/EAN: 9783741190650

Manufactured in Europe, USA, Canada, Australia, Japa

Cover: Foto ©Lupo / pixelio.de

Manufactured and distributed by brebook publishing software
(www.brebook.com)

Giuseppe Frassinetti

A dogmatic catechism

A

DOGMATIC CATECHISM.

FROM THE ITALIAN OF FRASSINETTI.

REVISED AND EDITED BY

THE OBLATE FATHERS OF ST. CHARLES.

WITH A PREFACE,

BY HIS GRACE

THE ARCHBISHOP OF WESTMINSTER.

R. WASHBOURNE, 18A, PATERNOSTER ROW.

1872.

INDEX.

	PAGE
THE PREFACE	ix
PREFACE TO THE SIXTH EDITION	xi
NOTICE	xiii

PROLOGUE.

OF RELIGION.

SECTION
I. The Necessity of a Religion — 1
II. The Necessity of a Revealed Religion — 2
III. The Marks of the Revealed Religion — 6

CHAPTER I.

THE SOURCES OF THEOLOGY.

I. Holy Scripture — 12
II. Tradition — 17
III. The Church — 20
IV. Councils — 32
V. The Roman Pontiff — 35
VI. The Holy Fathers, Doctors, and Schoolmen — 41
VII. History, Human Reason, and Philosophy — 43

CHAPTER II.

GOD ;— THE ONE AND TRINE.

I. General Idea of God — 45
II. The Immensity and Providence of God — 51

SECTION   PAGE
III. The Will of God, Predestination and Repro-
      bation - - - - - - - - - 55
IV. The Beatific Vision - - - - - - 63
V. The Mystery of the Most Blessed Trinity - 66

CHAPTER III.

GOD ;—THE CREATOR.

I. The Creation of the World ;—in general - - 73
II. The Angels - - - - - - - 75
III. Man - - - - - - - - 81
IV. Heaven, Purgatory and Hell - - - - 88
V. The Consummation of the World - - - 94

CHAPTER IV.

THE INCARNATION OF THE SON OF GOD.

I. General Idea of the Mystery - - - - 102
II. The Body and Soul of Christ - - - - 110
III. The different Titles which belong to Christ,
      the Worship due to Him, and the Worship
      proper to His Saints - - - - - 116

CHAPTER V.

THE GRACE OF CHRIST.

I. General Idea of the different kinds of Grace, and
      particularly of Actual Grace - - - - 121
II. Sanctifying Grace - - - - - - 129
III. The Merit of Good Works - - - - 134

CHAPTER VI.

THE THEOLOGICAL VIRTUES.

I. Idea of those Virtues in general - - - 139
II. The Virtue of Faith - - - - - 141
III. The Virtue of Hope - - - - - 154
IV. The Virtue of Charity - - - - - 158

CHAPTER VII.

THE SACRAMENTS.

SECTION   PAGE
  I. The Sacraments ;—in general -   -   -   - 168
 II. Baptism .   -   -   -   -   -   -   - 183
III. Confirmation -   -   -   -   -   -   - 194
 IV. The Holy Eucharist   -   -   -   -   - 196
  V. Penance -   -   -   -   -   -   -   - 208
     APPENDIX ON INDULGENCES   -   -   - 219
 VI. Extreme Unction -   -   -   -   -   - 221
VII. Order   -   -   -   -   -   -   -   - 223
VIII. Matrimony   -   -   -   -   -   -   - 226

APPENDIX.

ON THE MODE OF TEACHING CHRISTIAN DOCTRINE TO CHILDREN.

  I. The Importance of this teaching   .   -   - 228
 II. The Method to be observed in this teaching   - 229
III. The Maxims to be instilled into Children -   - 232
 IV. The qualifications which those who teach Children
         Christian Doctrine should endeavour to acquire 235

IMPORTANT INSTRUCTIONS FOR THE ADMINISTRATION OF THE HOLY SACRAMENTS TO THE SICK.

  I. Regarding Confession   -   -   -   -   - 238
 II. Regarding the Holy Viaticum -   -   -   - 238
III. Regarding Extreme Unction -   -   -   - 239

PROFESSION OF THE CATHOLIC FAITH   -   -   - 241

PREFACE.

THE translation into English of Frassinetti's Catechism is highly opportune. The Council of the Vatican most wisely decreed that a Lesser Catechism should be prepared for the use of the Faithful. What the Council of Trent provided in the " *Catechismus ad Parochos*" for the " *Ecclesia Docens*," the Council of the Vatican is providing for the " *Ecclesia Discens*." But, in decreeing that one authoritative text, in the form of a Catechism, should be prepared, the Council in no way limits, either the liberty of Bishops to frame Catechisms of a fuller and more explicit kind for the use of their dioceses, or that of Catechists to deliver such oral explanations as are suited to the capacities and needs of their people.

The Bishops of England, in a united Pastoral Letter, have enjoined the Clergy to renewed diligence and punctuality in their

office as Catechists. No one who knows the
condition of this country can fail to see the
need we have of expository Catechisms, rising
from the simple text of the penny Catechism
to such extensive works as Gaume's " *Cate-
chisme de Persévérance.*" The rapid development of intelligence in all classes renders the
office of the Catechist both more necessary,
and more difficult. It must never be forgotten
that a good Catechist is a preacher of a very
high order. The " traditio Symboli " is not
a mere repetition of question and answer, but
an elucidation of the doctrines of faith, which
affords full scope for the intelligence of a
theologian, and for the charity of a pastor.

The Catechism of Frassinetti is a good
example of what a Catechist may do. It is
singularly well adapted to the needs of our
middle class, for whom, as yet, a sufficient
provision has hardly been made. I therefore
very heartily recommend the use of this
Catechism to the Clergy and Faithful.

✠ Henry Edward,

Archbishop of Westminster.

Nativity of Our Lady, 1871.

PREFACE TO THE SIXTH EDITION.

PUBLISHED AT GENOA IN 1865.

THIS little work has been cordially received, not only here, but throughout Italy; all former editions are exhausted, and I now put forth this sixth edition, to which some additions have been made.

I published this compendium principally for the use of clerics, who might have to instruct children in Christian Doctrine, before they had themselves gone through the whole course of Dogmatic Theology. At the same time I had in view the profit of lay persons, who are often deficient in the knowledge of certain subjects, not easily found in the books which come in their way. The knowledge of these subjects is of especial importance in our days, because of the many errors so daringly scattered abroad among our people.

To such persons the "Prologue on the necessity of a Religion," the chapters on "The Grounds of Theology," "God the Creator," "The Grace of Christ," "The Theological Virtues," and, above all, on "The Virtue of Faith," will be especially useful.

These chapters contain observations of great importance, and such as are rarely met with in catechetical works. The "Important Instructions for the Administration of the Holy Sacraments to the Sick" will also be found useful.

The Method I have observed is as follows :— I prove the Dogma by arguments which will satisfy all Catholics ; then I state the theological opinions which refer to the Dogma itself, and which are commonly received in the schools. So that my reader, enlightened in regard to what he ought to hold as of Faith, and to embrace as agreeable to the truth, may easily guard himself from error, as well as from false or ill-grounded opinions.

I protest that I submit all my opinions, and every word I have written to the judgment of the Holy Roman Church: I glory in being her obedient son, and her interests I will promote to the utmost of my feeble power so long as I live.

NOTICE.

GIUSEPPE FRASSINETTI, the author of the following Catechism, was born at Genoa, on the 15th of December, 1803. He was the eldest son of Giambattista Frassinetti and his wife, Angela Viale, persons of moderate fortune, who however gave their children a good education, and consecrated them all to the Lord.

From his infancy he gave indications of talent and genius, along with a reflective disposition. In his studies, he excelled his companions, and made especial progress in Literature, Philosophy, and Theology. In the last he would have made his public disputation, as was the custom with the more distinguished students, had he not been prevented by the death of the Professor of Dogma.

His culture and learning, along with his conspicuous piety and practice, gave his friends the greatest hopes, when at length he was ordained priest. He was assiduous in all that becomes an ecclesiastic, in sacred studies, in the instruction of the young, and in the ministries of the house of God.

In his zeal for the salvation of his neighbour, he became a member of the congregation of *Evangelical Workers*, otherwise known as the *Fransonians*, who day and night gave themselves to preaching, catechizing, and the confessional; as well as of the *Urban Missionaries of St. Charles*, to whom was committed the conversion of those condemned to the galleys.

His facility, thus acquired, in the pulpit and the confessional, was of the greatest value to the parish of S. Pietro di Quinto, to which he was appointed, in spite of his youth. Here he sowed the seeds of an extraordinary devotion to, and frequentation of, the Sacraments, the best antidotes to infidelity and heresy, to which the people of that country were especially exposed, being given rather to navigation than to agriculture. He introduced the Perpetual Adoration of the Blessed Sacrament, and within two years was the means of assembling from that and the neighbouring parishes, no fewer than four thousand worshippers. He founded also a society of young women, which issued in the establishment of the Institute of St. Dorothea. In 1839, he was transferred to S. Sabina in Genoa, where he signalized himself by his diligence in the confessional, his ability and clearness in catechizing, and the excellence of his explanations of the gospel, and his sermons on Sundays and feast-days. He was especially celebrated for preaching during Novenas, and the Month of Mary; at other times he was wont to assemble the people in the evening for meditation, and to read to them some pious book. The visitation of the sick, the assistance of the dying, the succour of the poor, the care of those in peril of losing their innocence, the prevention of scandal, the consolation of the afflicted, and the correction, now loving and now severe, as occasion demanded, of the erring, were the matter of his daily thoughts and labours. His parishioners found in him a pastor of power, a master of virtue, meek, patient, and affable, careful in his conversation with women, profuse in giving, sober in his living, poor in apparel, and given to mortification.

For years he did not pass the gates of the city, took no recreation, and passed his days in study, prayer, and parochial labours. Deploring the general decay of faith, diminution of fervour, and relaxation of manners, he strove to arrest and remedy the evil by the dissemination of devout books and edifying literature; and by the formation of young men, girls, and ladies living in the world, into pious congregations for the promotion of their individual sanctification, and the practice of good works.

Besides the present Catechism, he wrote many valuable works which have been translated into French, Spanish, and German. Among them are the following :—" The Comfort of the Devout Soul," " Holy Virginity ;"—" the Jewel of Maidens," " Spiritual Exercises,—for the Young of Both Sexes," " Jesus Christ, the Rule of a Priest," " Devotion to Mary,—for the Young," " The Our Father of St. Theresa of Jesus," " A Treatise on Prayer,"—" The Rose without a Thorn," " Dialogues on the Commandments of the Church," " Two Hidden Joys," " The Art of Holiness," " Paradise on Earth," " An Hour of Holy Joy," " Words of Mary to Her Devout Clients," " The Twelve Stars," " Instructions on the Apostles' Creed," " A Life of St. Joseph;—in Seven Considerations,"and many others. The foregoing works are *opuscula*, and mainly intended for popular use, for which they are eminently adapted ; but to this learned, prudent, and holy priest, his brethren in the sacred ministry were no less indebted. For their use he wrote " The Young Parish Priest," and " The Compendium of the Moral Theology of St. Alphonsus di Liguori." This last took his intervals of leisure from parochial work during eighteen years. It was at first published in Latin, and had for its scope simply to give the mind of St. Alphonsus, without addition of his own. Subsequently he published it in Italian, with

the exception of certain portions, for obvious
reasons veiled in the language of the Church; and
this edition had notes and dissertations. It contained the fruits of long study and experience, and
was especially valuable as applying the moral law
to the various new questions to which changes in
the civil laws, the progress of commerce, and the
ever-varying manners and habits of the day gave
rise.

Frassinetti was engaged in preparing the fourth
edition of this work for the press, when he was
seized with his last illness. He did not, however,
it is believed, cease to say mass every day, until on
the 31st December, 1867, as he was making his
preparation for the Holy Sacrifice, he felt himself
unable to proceed, and was compelled to take to
his bed. His sickness speedily increased, and on
the second day of 1868 he died. He had been
conscious of his danger, and received the Last
Sacraments in full possession of his senses. No
sooner was his sickness known, than his door was
besieged by persons of all ranks; and after his
death his chamber was despoiled of almost all it
contained, by those who desired to carry away
some memorial of one so much admired and beloved. His funeral was celebrated with solemnity
amid the tears of his people; and an eulogium,
tender and eloquent, was pronounced by his stedfast

b

friend, and literary associate, the Canon and Professor Filippo Poggi.

Thus passed to his reward the holy priest, whose Dogmatic Catechism is now for the first time accessible in an English translation. It is, as its title implies, *dogmatic*, rather than controversial. It traverses briefly the whole cycle of Christian doctrine, and so covers more than those catechetical works which treat only of the points at issue between Catholics and Protestants. The Editors trust that it may prove of use to the many, who, from outside the Fold of Christ, are striving earnestly in their search after His Truth; as well as to those, who, having found it, desire to develop their knowledge in detail.

For the substance of this notice they have to express their grateful acknowledgments to Father Antonio Ballerini, S.J., Professor of Moral Theology in the Roman College, and the friend of Frassinetti. He writes; and his words will commend the work to all who know him : " I rejoice in the diffusion of the writings of this excellent priest. In my poor judgment, they combine solid doctrine with a quality rarely to be found, that of adaptation to the capacities of all. There is in them an union of devotion and spiritual affectionateness with discretion, in no way inferior to the sweet spirit of St. Francis de Sales."

To this testimony, they need only add that of the Reigning Pontiff Pius IX., who in a Brief directed, in 1863, to Sister Paola, Superioress of the Institute of St. Dorothea, speaks of Frassinetti as —"a priest SPECTATÆ DOCTRINÆ ET VIRTUTIS."

St. Mary of the Angels, Bayswater, London.
    Feast of St. Charles, 1871.

A

DOGMATIC CATECHISM.

PROLOGUE.

RELIGION.

SECT. I. *The Necessity of a Religion.*

Is it necessary for men to have a Religion?

A. Taking for granted the certainty of the existence of God, which no one who uses his reason can doubt, it is necessary for men to have a Religion; that is to say, that they should offer worship to the Supreme Being, who is God, from whom they derive existence and all blessings.

Why do you say that no one who uses his reason can doubt the existence of God, for many philosophers have not only doubted, but denied it: and they were men, who, besides being very learned, were most acute critics, and profound reasoners?

A. No true philosopher, that is to say, no good reasoner, even among Pagans, has ever doubted the existence of God. A few only, who, notwithstanding the acuteness of their intellects, abandoned themselves to every kind of infamy and crime, fearing God's chastisements, and not choosing to

amend their lives, sought to persuade themselves
that there was no God, so as, if possible, to arrive
at being impious without fear and remorse.   They
therefore blasphemously asserted that there is no
God.   But none the less were they persuaded that
He exists.   In fact, after having in their life-time
blasphemously denied God, in the hour of death,
either in penitence or in despair, they confessed
that there is a God.   As a sick man, to whom the
thought of death is grievous, seeks to persuade
himself that he will recover from his sickness,
however clear the reasons may be which should
convince him to the contrary ; so did these impious
philosophers, to whom the thought of the existence
of a God was intensely obnoxious, seek to persuade
themselves that there is no God, although they
had the clearest evidence of His existence.

Assuming the existence of God, why is it necessary that men should offer worship to this Supreme
Being ?

A. For the same reason that a son should love
his father, that a subject should pay homage to his
king, that one who has received benefits should be
grateful to his benefactor, &c.   This Supreme
Being is our Father, our King, and our Sovereign
Benefactor.

SECT. II.   *The Necessity of a Revealed Religion.*

Is natural religion sufficient, that is to say,
a worship given to God according to the dictates of

mere human reason; or is a determinate worship, manifested to us directly by God, by means of a supernatural revelation, requisite?

A. Mere human reason is not sufficient to make known to us all the truths necessary to the right knowledge of God. Human reason of itself cannot determine by what sacrifices, and with what rites man should acknowledge His supreme dominion, and honour Him. Moreover, of itself it is not able to determine all the laws of moral rectitude. Omitting all the other arguments which might be brought forward, it is sufficient to observe that this proposition is an undeniable fact. None of the philosophers who have treated of God and His attributes by the light of natural reason alone, attained to giving a just idea of the Supreme Being; and whilst they all agreed that He was to be honoured and adored, they were never able to agree as to the kind of sacrifices and rites which ought to be adopted.* The laws of morals, when left in the hands of mere philosophers, ever inclined either on one side or on the other, to what was unjust and base. The Pagan philosophers among the Greeks recognized the necessity of a revelation, and constantly looked for, and desired it. †

* What Rousseau himself wrote of Deist philosophers may be appropriately quoted here. "If we consider their reasons we shall find that they all tend to destroy—they agree only in mutual contradiction."

† Here are Plato's sentiments in the Dialogues with Alcibiades. "Socrates.—The safest course is to wait

It would seem that, as human reason became perfected, it might attain a point which it had not yet reached ; that is to say, a thorough knowledge of the divine attributes, of the most acceptable modes of honouring God, and of all the rules of the moral law ; and now that, in consequence of the march of enlightenment, human reason is near this perfection, we shall henceforth no longer stand in need of a supernatural revelation.

A. Considering the many centuries during which

---

patiently, and we certainly must wait until he come who shall instruct us in our duties towards God and towards men. ALCIBIADES.—When will that hour come, and who shall instruct us in these things? I ardently desire to behold this teacher ! SOCRATES.—He of whom we are speaking has care of thy concerns, but, as I think, he acts in regard to us, as Homer relates that Minerva acted with Diomed. Minerva dispelled the mists which darkened the eyes of Diomed, and he then saw the objects which were before him. In like manner it is necessary that a dense mist should be taken away from the eyes of thy understanding, in order that thou shouldest discern good from evil, which at present thou canst not do. ALCIBIADES.—Oh ! that he would come ! Oh ! that he would dissipate this darkness ! For my part, I would be ready to do whatever he should command, so that I might but become better than I am. SOCRATES.—This is what we ought to do, because in our ignorance we know not what sacrifices are pleasing to God and what are displeasing to Him. ALCIBIADES.—When that day shall arrive, our sacrifices will happily be pleasing to God, and I trust in His goodness that this day cannot be far off." You see how even Pagan philosophers desired a revealed religion, and acknowledged its necessity.

philosophers have studied how to bring the faculties
of the human mind to perfection, were our reason
capable of an absolute perfection, it would by this
time be perfect, and we should know all things, so
to speak, better than the angels ; but instead of this,
the republic of philosophers (I speak of those only
who disdain the light of revelation) does but find
itself in greater confusion, and greater darkness ; so
that there is no doubt but that twenty centuries ago,
Plato, Aristotle, and other heathens, taught a philosophy far more reasonable, correct and moral, than
that taught by the infidel philosophers of the present
day.   Man has in his nature a depth of malice and
ignorance which is unfathomable ; and if he would
really perfect his spiritual faculties, he must join
the light of revelation to the light of reason.   Moreover, it is not for us to judge of the progress of
enlightenment in our own age ; future ages will
judge of it dispassionately and without self-love.
We may believe that it will not be denied its just
meed of praise for progress in the industrial
sciences ; we may doubt whether it will secure
equal praise for progress in metaphysical and moral
science.   Meanwhile, we challenge our infidel
philosophers to come to some agreement amongst
themselves ; for, whilst we are deafened by the
confused warfare of a multitude of irreconcileable
systems, we cannot even understand what they say
to us.   Let them agree among themselves, and then
we may begin to entertain the supposition that they

are capable of perfecting human reason. Whilst the tumultuous chaos of their opinions does but deepen more and more, what can we believe, what can we say? Therefore the ridiculous hope of the complete perfection of human reason cannot exempt us from acknowledging the necessity of a revealed religion, which may instruct us in the knowledge of God, in the way in which we are to adore Him, and in the rules of true morality.

Sect. III. *The Marks of the Revealed Religion.*

Many are the religions in the world, which claim to have been revealed by God; but since they are all opposed one to the other, they cannot all have been revealed; one alone can have been revealed by God, and how are we to distinguish it from the rest?

A. Most certainly God, who is the Truth, cannot reveal as true, things contrary one to another, each of which supposes the falsehood of the rest; and so amongst all the so-called revealed religions one alone can be the offspring of a true revelation. No abstruse researches nor prolix demonstrations are needful to distinguish this one from the rest. As a precious diamond is distinguished amidst the fragments of brittle glass, so is the true revealed religion distinguished from those which are false. The religions which call themselves Revealed Religions are, Paganism, Mahometanism, Judaism, and Christianity. Paganism, which is a huge collection, or,

to speak more correctly, a huge chaos, of innumerable worships, is repugnant to reason, because, we
may say, that of everything it makes a god. So
that, according to its dictates, that which in one
place is the god to whom victims are to be sacrificed, is in another place the victim which is to be
sacrificed to, as a god. In Egypt, sacrifices were
offered to the ox; in Greece, it was the ox that was
offered in sacrifice. One of the ancients relates
that, in a certain place, the very priests disputed
among themselves, which of two animals was the
victim to be sacrificed,—which the god to whom
the sacrifice was to be made. This religion has all
the marks of folly, and none of divinity. Nor has
Mahometanism anything divine about it; no
prophecies verified, no miracles wrought; born in
ignorance and nurtured in ignorance, it was established and propagated solely by the power of the
sword. Barbarity is its support, uncleanness is its
food, and both together, all it hopes for in the life
to come; never was there a sage who did not abhor
it, and hold it in derision. But of Judaism we must
speak in a different way. Judaism can boast of
prophecies fulfilled, and miracles performed; its
books are holy, and have impressed on them the
character of divinity; therefore the Jewish religion
is a religion revealed by God. But this religion
was not intended to endure for ever; it was to give
place to that religion of which it was but the figure.
Its books say clearly that God would make to Him-

self a new people, who should possess a new law, and a new sacrifice; therefore the Jewish religion was that worship by which God chose once to be honoured by men; but it is so no longer. And truly wonderful is the abandonment, in which God has left it ;—without a temple, without a priesthood, without sacrifices, and, more than this, without a country; so that the Jews, dispersed over all the world, are strangers in every land. . The Jewish religion therefore, of itself, declares that it is no longer that religion which is pleasing to God, but that Christianity has been substituted in its place. Christianity is now the one and only religion which has the marks of divinity, and it alone will bear them to the end of the world. All the prophecies of Holy Scripture confirm its truth. Infinite miracles attest that Christianity is the work of God. The Christian religion is that which gives to men the grandest and most perfect idea of the Supreme Being, which it is possible for them to have; it teaches a most sublime way in which He is to be adored; it prescribes moral laws, all based on justice and holiness; and so the most ignorant Christian, if he be but instructed in the first rudiments of his faith, is more learned in divinity, in worship, and in morals, than any philosopher whatsoever, not a Christian. It suffices but to know the Christian religion, in order to feel compelled to proclaim it to be the true, the only religion which enjoys the marks of divine revelation.

How comes it that, since Christianity bears all the marks of revelation, it should be the most opposed of all religions ?

A. You must observe from whom the opposition comes; because, from the quality of the enemy, we may recognise the quality of the object of his attack. The Christian religion was always more opposed than any of the other religions which are in the world, but it was always opposed by the impious and the impure. The persecutors of the Christian religion, as history shows us, were always the most lost in vice ; and the more fierce among them were always monsters of crime and infamy. What wonder is it that the wicked should hate that which is good, and hate it the more, the greater it is ? Meanwhile this continued opposition, whilst it constitutes the glory of Christianity, furnishes us with another mark of its divinity ; for, whilst it has been the most opposed of all religions, it is at the same time the grandest and the most unchangeable. After twenty centuries of strife it is still the same, full of force and vigour, spreading itself triumphantly over the whole world, and changing its enemies into its children, so soon as it becomes known to them. This fact, over and above the promise of God, assures us of its indefectibility.

But in the Christian religion there are many sects opposed one to another ; which of these is the true one ?

A. Not one of those sects ; all are false. The

true religion is that which is no sect; that which
was founded by the Apostles, which has their faith
and their customs; that which all sects oppose;
that which spreads itself over the whole world, em-
braces all ages, and therefore calls itself, and is in
truth, the Catholic religion. All sects have for their
heads, men who are deserters from the religion of
Christ and the Apostles; therefore they can be
called Christian sects, only in so far as that they
acknowledge Christ, and pretend to honour Him after
their fashion. But they cannot be called Christian,
in the sense of making part of that religion which
was truly founded by Christ. Facts demonstrate
that they are separated from it, because they fight
against it. Of such sects we shall speak in chap. i.
sect. iii.*

* The unreasonableness of indifference in the matter of
religion will be clear and manifest if we reflect sincerely on
the subjects here briefly mentioned. If God ought to be
honoured by a worship, if He has revealed what that worship
is which He wills to receive from us, if in manifesting it to
us, He warns us that every other worship is henceforth an
abomination to Him : this being one of the fundamental
truths of the Catholic religion, how is it possible we should
believe that God is indifferent as to what kinds of worship
there may be on the earth? Can it be reasonable to suppose
that God esteems Himself honoured equally by chaste and
pure worship, and by the impure and abominable rites of
paganism? Can we imagine that the slaughter of the twenty
thousand human victims who were annually sacrificed in
idolatrous Mexico, when the breasts of those miserable beings
were torn open in order to pluck thence their still living, palpi-

CHAPTER I.

THE SOURCES OF THEOLOGY.

THE sources of theology are the springs whence the necessary arguments are taken, both to prove and elucidate the truths of the faith and the principles and rules of morals, and to defend those truths and rules from the sophisms of heretics, or of bad Catholics.

---

tating hearts, was as pleasing to Him as the innocent and pious sacrifice of our altars? Can we suppose that the groans and shrieks of horrible despair which rang through those halls of terror and death, pleased Him as much as the peaceful hymns, breathing gratitude and love, which resound in our temples? It seems to me a lesser evil to suppose that God does not exist, than to suppose the existence of a God so stupid and insensate as he would be, who should hold himself equally honoured by all and every kind of worship that ever has been, and is now, in the world.

Here we will give the propositions condemned in the Syllabus annexed to the Encyclical of the 8th December, 1864, sect. iii., in order to make known the errors which they condemn.

"XV. Every man is free to embrace and profess that religion which, by the guidance of the light of reason, he shall judge to be true.

"XVI. In the exercise of any religion whatsoever, men may find the way of eternal life, and gain eternal salvation.

"XVII. We may at least entertain a good hope of the eternal salvation of all those who are not in the true Church of Christ.

"XVIII. Protestantism is but a different form of the same

These sources or grounds are ten in number :—
1. Holy Scripture; 2. Tradition; 3. The Consent
of the Church Catholic; 4. Councils; 5. The
Judgments of the Roman Pontiff; 6. The Authority
of the Holy Fathers ; 7. The Authority of the Doctors and Schoolmen ; 8. The Authority of History ;
9. The Authority of Human Reason; 10. The
Authority of Philosophy.   This is the common
teaching of theologians.

Sect. I.   Holy Scripture.

What is meant under the name of Holy Scripture ?
A. The Holy Bible, which comprises all those
divine books, to the number of seventy-two, which,
by the sacred Council of Trent (Sess. 4) are recognised as having been inspired by God to their

---

true Christian religion, in which equally as in the Catholic
Church, men can please God."
  The Catholic Christian must believe precisely the contrary of that which these condemned propositions set forth.
  The third proposition condemned in the above-mentioned
Encyclical must also be noted ; as in it the following error, or
rather errors, are confuted : "Liberty of conscience and of
worship is the proper right of every man, and in every well-
constituted society it ought to be proclaimed and established
by law ; every citizen has the right of perfect freedom in
manifesting and declaring openly and in public, by word of
mouth and in print, or in any other way, his own opinions,
whatever they may be, unrestricted by any authority ecclesiastical or civil."

authors, and written by them with such assistance of the Holy Spirit, as that they could not have inserted therein the very smallest error, whether out of malice, or from human weakness.

How is Holy Scripture divided?

A. It is divided into the Old and New Testaments. The Old Testament contains all the sacred books written before the Incarnation of the Son of God, beginning with Genesis, and ending with the Second Book of Maccabees; the New Testament contains those which were written after the Incarnation, beginning with the Gospel of St. Matthew, and ending with the Apocalypse of St. John.

There cannot, of course, be errors in those books, the authors of which were inspired by God; but there might be errors in the Latin Bible which we make use of, seeing that this is not the original, but is entirely a translation from the Hebrew and Greek texts? *

A. The Church has made use of this Bible for more than twelve centuries; were it corrupted or changed in any important particular, Jesus Christ could not have permitted His Church so to make use of it, without failing in that assistance which He promised her, and which renders her infallible. The sacred Council of Trent (Sess. 4) even declares him excommunicated who does not believe any

* Some pretend that the Epistle of St. Paul to the Romans was written in Latin.

one, or any part of any one of the said sacred books which are contained in our Latin ; Bible which is also called the Vulgate of St. Jerome, because that most learned and holy Father is the author of the greater part of this version.

But would it not be safer to trust to the ancient original texts, rather than to our Vulgate ?

A. Whatever may be the state of the original texts at the present day, it is certain that they have not been revised and corrected by the Church in the same way as our Vulgate ; therefore, in matters concerning faith and morals, our Vulgate ought really to be preferred to the original texts.

Have the words of Holy Scripture one meaning, or several meanings ?

A. Very many words and sentences of Holy Scripture have two meanings ; that is to say, a literal meaning and a mystical meaning. The literal meaning is that which the words present of themselves ; the mystical meaning, on the contrary, is that which the things present which are signified by the words. For example : Holy Scripture narrates that Abraham had two sons—one by Agar, a bond-woman, the other by Sara, a free woman. The literal sense is, that Abraham had Ishmael by Agar his servant whom he had taken to wife, and that afterwards he had Isaac by Sara; who was also his wife, and who was born of the same particular family from which he himself sprang : the mystical sense is, that God, figured in Abraham, had two peoples who worshipped Him, the one in bondage under the Mosaic law—that is, the Jewish people—the other free under the Gospel law—that is ourselves, the people of Christ. So the Holy Fathers explain St. Paul (Gal. iv.).

There is still another sense, which is called—accommodated. What is that?

A. We call that the accommodated sense, when a sentence of Holy Scripture which expresses some determinate truth, is made use of to express another to which it may be applied. Thus, the Church uses in praise of Most Holy Mary, various encomiums applied by Scripture to the Divine Wisdom; as for example, the following words: "I am the Mother of fair love, and of fear, and of knowledge, and of holy hope" (Ecclesiasticus xxiv. 24).

May we trust to our own judgment alone, in the understanding and interpretation of Holy Scripture?

A. The Catholic, Apostolic and Roman Church is the depositary of Holy Scripture. She alone may judge definitively of the true senses of the sacred books; she desires, however, that in the understanding and interpretation of them we should follow the unanimous judgment of the Holy Fathers (Council of Trent, Sess. 4), who are the depositaries of tradition, and who were specially assisted by God in the interpretation and understanding of them. It should be noted that all heresies have sprung from the desire to interpret Holy Scripture according to the private judgment of individuals.

" No heresies have sprung up, save when the Scriptures, which are good, were not well understood " (St. Aug. on St. John, chap. xviii.).

Would it not be well to make translations of the Bible into the vulgar tongue, so that it might be put into the hands of all, even of the laity ?

A. The Church forbids that the Bible, literally translated into the vulgar tongue, should be given to be read by all persons indifferently. She even forbids absolution of sins to be given to those who choose to read it, or retain possession of it without permission. The proof that it cannot be a good thing to put the Bible into the hands of all persons is, that being full of mysteries it would injure rather than profit the ignorant ; and this is manifest from the zeal with which Protestants scatter abroad, everywhere and at great expense, an incredible number of vernacular translations of the Bible. Moreover, the Sacred Congregation of the Index, in a decree dated the 13th June, 1757, prohibits " All translations of the Bible in the vulgar tongue, unless they have been approved by the Apostolic See, or edited with notes taken from the Fathers of the Church, or from learned and Catholic writers." Further, this decree was renewed in the Monitum of the Congregation of the Index, fer. v. die 7 Januarii, 1836.

This applies even to translations of the Bible in the vulgar tongue made by Catholic authors, and faithfully following the Vulgate, such as that of

Monsignor Martini, printed without notes.* Hence we may understand how rigorously prohibited are the translations made by Protestants, changed and mutilated as they are, and wanting in whole books. Such are Diodati's Bibles, which are scattered abroad by the Bible Societies, with the hope, but we trust the vain hope, of protestantising Italy. Those Bibles especially may neither be bought, nor received as a gift, nor read, nor kept possession of, by any one.

Sect. II. *Tradition.*

What is Tradition, properly so called, as constituting one of the sources of theology ?

* Of the edition, however, published by Monsignor Martini, with notes, His Holiness Pius VI., in a letter to that prelate, in April, 1778, writes : "You judge exceedingly well that the faithful should be entitled to the reading of the Holy Scriptures : for these are the most abundant sources, which ought to be left open to every one, to draw from them purity of morals and of doctrine, and to eradicate the errors which are so widely disseminated in these corrupt times. This you have seasonably effected, as you declare, by publishing the Sacred Writings in the language of your country, suitable to every one's capacity ; especially when you show and set forth that you have added explanatory notes which, being extracted from the holy Fathers, preclude every possible danger of abuse. Thus you have not swerved either from the laws of the Congregation of the Index, or from the Constitution published on this subject by Benedict XIV." As to the Catholic translations in English, they may be read by all the faithful, as appears from the approbations of the bishops prefixed to them.—Ed.

A. According to the sense of the holy Fathers and the holy Council of Trent, (Sess. 4) by Tradition is to be understood those doctrines which the inspired authors did not originally commit to writing, and which may, or may not, have been since written.

How are the Traditions divided?

A. Of the Traditions of the Evangelical Law, of which we are now speaking, some are called Divino-Apostolic Traditions; and some, Apostolic Traditions. The Divino-Apostolic Traditions are divided into traditions that regard dogma, and into traditions that regard morals. The first comprise the truths taught by Jesus Christ to His Apostles, or revealed to them after His ascension into heaven. Among this number may be placed the dogma that there are seven sacraments of the new law, neither more nor less. The Traditions that regard morals, that is, practice, comprise the precepts or commandments given by Jesus Christ to His Apostles. Amongst them may be reckoned the rites essential to the administration of the sacraments, and which, if changed as to their substance, would render the sacraments invalid. For instance, in the form of the sacrament of penance, were the priest to say, I wash thee from thy sins, instead of saying, I absolve thee. These Divino-Apostolic Traditions, both as regards dogma and practice, are unchangeable, and constitute an irrefragable source of theology. The simply Apostolic Traditions comprise the constitutions framed by the Apostles, as Pastors of the Church, for a sound rule of discipline. Among these may be placed the fast of Lent. Such Traditions are changeable; so that the Supreme Pontiff, as Universal Pastor, may make changes in them as he deems expedient.

Must the Traditions of the Church be necessarily admitted?

A. It is a dogma defined by the holy Council of Trent that there are traditions (sess. 4, and elsewhere). This must necessarily be admitted; because all that is to be believed and practised is not found in the books of the Bible. We do not find in the Bible that the sacraments of the new law are seven; therefore without tradition we could not believe that dogma. In like manner the forms of the different sacraments are not found in the divine books; therefore without tradition they could not be administered. For ¡this cause St. Paul said: "Hold the traditions; Tenete traditiones" (2 Thess. ii. 14.) Moreover all heretics, as Canus points out, reject Tradition, because they recognize in it a weapon even more fitted to defeat them than Holy Scripture itself; for by interpreting Scripture according to their own fashion, they twist it to their own meaning, but Tradition does not depend upon interpretations.

SECT. III. *The Church.*

How do you define the Church of Christ?

A. The true Church of Christ on Earth—not to speak of the Church Triumphant, which is the union of the blessed in heaven,—nor yet of the Church Suffering, which is the union of just souls detained in purgatory;—the true Church of Christ on earth that is, the Church Militant, is the union of all the faithful, who communicate one with another, by profession of the same faith, by the participation of the same sacraments, and who are subject to their own Bishops, and in especial to the Roman Pontiff, who is the centre of all Catholic union. Such is the definition common to theologians.

What persons do not belong to the Church of Christ?

A. Those who have not yet received baptism; and therefore, not infidels only, but even catechumens, although they believe all the revealed truths of the holy faith, do not belong to the Church. Heretics, that is to say, those who belong to some sect which does not believe all the dogmas of the faith, do not belong to it.* Schismatics, that is to say, those who refuse to submit to their own lawful pastors, and, still more, to the authority of the Roman Pontiff, do not belong to it. Excommunicated persons also who are notoriously and publicly declared such, do not belong to it.

* All Protestants are heretics.

Are there then excommunicated persons who do belong to the Church?

A. Of right, no excommunicated person belongs to the Church; but by indulgence or permission of the Church herself, such excommunicated persons as are called tolerated, that is, such as are not publicly declared excommunicated, belong to it. In like manner secret heretics, that is, such persons as, without declaring themselves for any sect in particular, secretly gainsay some Catholic dogma, whilst they affect to be united to the Church, and subject to their lawful pastors, belong to it. Such men, however, belong not to the soul, but to the body of the Church, in the same way that a withered member sometimes remains united to the body from which it derives neither vigour nor life.

Has it not been said by some, that imperfect Christians do not belong to the Church?

A. There were a few heretics who pretended that the Church was composed of perfect Christians only; but this was to destroy and annihilate the Church, for on this earth none were ever found perfect, properly so called, except the Most Blessed Virgin, who, preserved from original sin, was also free from every imperfection : other saints are called perfect, not because they really were so, but because they constantly aspired after perfection,* and

* A continual striving after perfection is reputed perfection. (*St. Bernard*).

with every possible endeavour, sought to strip themselves of their imperfections.

Are those to be considered as belonging to the Church, who are in a state of mortal sin?

A. Without doubt; nay! this is an article of the faith, and the contrary error was condemned in various propositions of Quesnel by the Bull Unigenitus.

Do reprobate Catholics, that is those whom God foresees will be damned because of their iniquities, belong to the Church?

A. It is an article of the faith that they belong to it. The contrary error was also condemned by the said Bull Unigenitus.

What are the marks of the Church of Christ?

A. They are four, as enumerated in the Niceno-Constantinopolitan Creed. The Church is One, is Holy, is Catholic, and is Apostolic.

Explain to me the first mark.

A. The true Church is One, especially by the unity of her Head, which is Christ; by the unity of the means which lead her to her end, which is eternal salvation; by the unity of her one and the same spiritual food, which is the Body and Blood of Jesus Christ; by the unity of one and the same faith, of one and the same hope, of one and the same Spirit who directs and governs her.

Who is the origin and centre of this unity which the Church has on earth?

A. Following the authority of all the Holy Fathers,

all Catholics are agreed that the origin and centre of this unity is the Roman Pontiff; that he has a primacy of honour, jurisdiction and authority over all the various churches of the earth, which all, united under this head constituted by Jesus Christ, form one sole Church. Take away this centre of unity, and they would be so many separate churches, and no longer one Church.

Explain to me the second mark.

A. The true Church is Holy, especially by the holiness of her Head, which is Christ; by the holiness of her sacraments, of her faith, and of her morals; by the holiness also of the more excellent of her members, who are the just; and by the holiness of her rites.

Explain to me the third mark.

A. The true Church is Catholic, that is—universal, because she extends through all times, and will last to the end of the world; because she extends over all places, being spread abroad in all the parts of the earth; and because she gathers all nations within her fold.

Explain to me the fourth mark.

A. The true Church is Apostolic, because she was founded by the Apostles, because she preserves their doctrine, and because their successors are her legitimate pastors.

What are the properties of this Church ?

A. They are three. She is visible, indefectible, and infallible.

Are those properties necessary to her?

A. Their necessity is manifest. The Church of Christ is the only true religion in the world, and those only who belong to her can obtain eternal life; therefore it is necessary that she be visible, in order that those who are not in this Church may recognize her, and may seek to enter within her fold. It is necessary that she be indefectible, because if the Church could fail, even for a short time, during that time it would be made an impossibility for men to save their souls. It is necessary that she be infallible, because if she could err, she could not securely lead her children to the attainment of their end—of eternal salvation.

In what matters is the Church infallible?

A. She is infallible in matters of faith and morals. So that when she declares that any truth appertains to the faith, and when she approves or disapproves of any practice appertaining to morals, it is impossible that she should err.

What renders her infallible?

A. The assistance of the Holy Spirit, who by a special providence governs her, and moreover speaks to men by means of her.

To what Church do the foresaid marks and properties belong?

A. To the Roman Church; not simply as Roman, that is, as restricted within the limits of the territory of the diocese of Rome; but as she is the universal Church, which has for its head and supreme pastor the Roman Pontiff. For this reason, not now only, but in the first ages of Christianity, to say Roman Christians, and to say Catholics, was one and the selfsame thing.

What must we say, then, of the Protestant churches, who also claim to be called Holy, Catholic, and Apostolic ?

A. They call themselves so with as much right as Italians would have to call themselves French. When they were united to the Roman Church, they really made part of the Holy, Catholic, and Apostolic Church ; but now they are neither Holy, nor Catholic, nor Apostolic. They are not Holy; because they have no longer Jesus Christ for their Head, who is the source of all holiness ; and they sometimes authorise dogmas and morals which are not holy. They are not Catholic ; because they do not extend throughout all times, and are restricted to some particular province or kingdom. They are not Apostolic ; because their founders were not the successors of the Apostles, but deserters from the Church founded by the Apostles, and enemies of their doctrine ; and in the same way that Italians, if they chose to call themselves French, would find none, either friends or enemies, to give them that name, so Protestants will never find any one who will give to their Churches the names of Holy, Catholic, Apostolic. They must be content with their own names, and to be called the Lutheran Church, the Calvinist Church, the Zuinglian Church, the Anglican Church, &c.

What must we say of the schismatical Greek Churches ?

A. Inasmuch as they are schismatical—that is, separated and divided from the Holy, Catholic, and Apostolic Church—they do not belong to her. Moreover, they are also heretical, because they deny several dogmas of the faith ; and, amongst others, that the Holy Spirit proceeds, as from the Father, so also from the Son. Observe that although these Churches, separated from Catholic unity, are called by many by the name of Greek or Eastern Churches, they ought to be called simply Protestant, because in opposing dogmas defined by the Church, they protest against the Church, as is clearly pointed out by Count De Maistre.

We have seen that the Church is infallible in her decisions regarding faith and morals. Now, supposing some controversy should arise, to whom does the definition belong ?

A. Observe that in the Church we must dis- ' tinguish two parts. The teaching Church and the hearing Church. The Sovereign Pontiff, with the other bishops, forms the teaching Church ; the whole of the rest of the Christian people, priests not excepted, forms the hearing Church. It belongs, therefore, to the Sovereign Pontiff and the bishops to define questions which may arise in regard to faith or morals.

Can any particular bishop define such questions ?

A. Certainly not; but the body of bishops united with the Roman Pontiff can definitively determine such questions; and this agreement is made by means of a General Council, or by means of a Pontifical Bull, accepted by the whole body of bishops. It is not, however, necessary that all the bishops should accept it; it is sufficient that it be received, or not opposed, by the majority; and in such case bishops who should dissent and refuse to submit themselves, would become schismatics and heretics. You must carefully note that all this is of faith,* as all Catholic theologians agree.

How must we answer heretics who maintain that Scripture is the judge of all controversies regarding faith and morals?

* Since the date of the Vatican Council it is now also certain, by the certainty of Catholic faith, what before and always was certain by certainty of theological demonstration, that the Supreme Pontiff, apart from the bishops, and by himself, is infallible in his definition of questions of faith and morals. The Council teaches and defines: "That the Roman Pontiff, when he speaks *ex Cathedrâ*—that is, when, exercising his office of pastor and teacher of all Christians, in accordance with his supreme apostolic authority, he defines a doctrine as to faith and morals, to be held by the Universal Church,— has, through the Divine assistance, promised to him in Blessed Peter, that Infallibility wherewith the Divine Redeemer willed His Church to be endowed in defining doctrine as to faith and morals; and therefore, that such definitions of the Roman Pontiff are, of themselves, and not from the consent of the Church, irreformable."—*Fourth Session, July 18th, 1870. First Dogmatic Constitution on the Church of Christ,* chap. iv.—ED.

A. You must answer that Holy Scripture serves
as a rule by which errors are condemned, and truths
defined; but that Holy Scripture itself neither defines nor condemns.   Every state has a body of
laws; but would it not be a ridiculous thing to sup-
press the tribunals, and expect the laws to condemn
the guilty and to absolve the innocent?   Holy
Scripture is the code of the Church; but the Church
is the tribunal to whom it belongs to define the
meaning of her code.   It pleases heretics to esta-
blish Holy Scripture as the judge in all controversies; because, by explaining it according to their
caprice, they may say that the judgment is in their
favour, and they are not afraid that Holy Scripture
should ever summon a council, or issue a bull to
condemn them.

They say further that every one may judge all
controversies by his own private judgment, enlightened in the understanding of Holy Scripture by
the Holy Spirit?

A. Were it true that the Holy Spirit enlightens
the minds of all Christians, so that no one could
err in the understanding of Holy Scripture, there
would never have been controversies in such
matters; hence we must say that He does not en-
lighten all, and does not render all infallible.
Which, then, are the private judgments illuminated by the Holy Spirit?   How shall we distinguish them from those which He has not illuminated?
And further, if heretics are illuminated by the Holy   ·

Spirit to decide controversies according to their private judgment, they must needs make the Holy Spirit the author of those innumerable contradictions which divide them into a thousand sects, and make a chaos of their faith or religion.

What shall we say of those who give authority to decide controversies to the general multitude of the Christian people ?

A. This is pure delirium in matters of faith. We may admit it when we see the sheep leading their shepherds to pasture. Jesus Christ said to the Apostles, Teach ye all nations. He did not say this to the multitude.

May not the decision of religious controversies be assigned to the temporal sovereign ?

A. From the very fact that the authority of sovereigns is temporal, it does not extend to religious controversies, which are spiritual. Jesus Christ gave the keys to St. Peter, not to the kings or to the emperors. In a word, be well assured that to give authority to determine religious controversies to any, save only to the Church, and to those who represent her, is an error against the faith which no Catholic would ever take upon himself to defend.

Can the Church make laws which will bind the consciences of the faithful ?

A. There is no doubt of it ; and all the councils and the bulls of the Sovereign Pontiffs prove it. Both the one and the other are full of laws which

are always observed by good Christians.   Besides,
no society can subsist without laws which shall rule
and direct the actions of its members.   Now the
Church is a society ; and so without laws to rule
and direct the actions of her members, she could
not subsist.

Have the laws of the Church force and vigour
without the approbation and sanction of the civil
government ?

A. Undoubtedly the laws of the Church have
force and vigour of themselves, independently of
any approbation or sanction whatsoever of civil
governments.   We have new proof of this in the
condemnation of the following propositions, proscribed in the Encyclical of 8th December, 1864 :—

" 10. The laws of the Church do not bind in
conscience, except when they are promulgated by
the civil power.

" 11. It is necessary that the acts and decrees of
the Roman pontiffs concerning religion and the
Church, should have the approbation and sanction,
or at least the assent, of the civil power.

" 12. The apostolic constitutions by which secret
societies are condemned (whether the oath of secresy
be exacted in them, or be not exacted), and by which
their followers and abettors are excommunicated,
has no force whatever in those countries where
such assemblies are tolerated by the civil government."

" 17. The ecclesiastical power is not, of divine

right, distinct from and independent of the civil power, nor can such distinction and independence be maintained without invasion and usurpation by the Church of the essential rights of the civil power."

The errors contained in these propositions are reproved, proscribed, and condemned; and the Sovereign Pontiff wills and commands that they be regarded as such by all the children of the Catholic Church.

Can the Church decree anything which binds the consciences of the faithful in order to the use of temporal things, if those temporal things have regard to spiritual things; as for example, were she to punish the invaders of ecclesiastical property with excommunication?

A. It is certain that the Church has such a right and power; of this right and power she has need for her spiritual interests; and although in the abstract these are diverse and distinct from temporal interests, nevertheless, in practice, they are so closely allied with them, that it would be impossible for her to promote the former, if she were hindered her guardianship of the latter. In this world spiritual things have need of material things, as the soul has need of the body. The sacraments themselves, the very dogmas of the faith, have need of material objects: one sacrament needs water; another, bread and wine; another, oil, &c. The dogmas of faith need paper on which they may be

written and by which they may be transmitted un-
changed from generation to generation. It is clear
that her ministers need food and raiment; that the
Churches need objects appropriated to worship,
&c. It is clear, therefore, that the Church could
not promote her spiritual interests if she could not
also guard her temporal or material interests. The
Church, then, having the right and the power to
guard her temporal interests, inasmuch as they are
necessary to her spiritual interests, it follows, as a
consequence, that she can bind the consciences of
the faithful in order to the use of temporal things,
where such temporal things have regard to spiritual
things. This is proved by the condemnation of the
following propositions, which are proscribed by the
same Encyclical as those above-mentioned :—

" 14. The Church may decree nothing which can
bind the consciences of the faithful in order to the
use of temporal things."

" 13. The excommunication fulminated by the
Council of Trent and by the Roman pontiffs against
those who invade and usurp the rights and property
of the Church, is based on the confusion of spiritual
with civil and political order, in the sole pursuit of a
worldly good."

Sect. IV. *Councils.*

How do you define an Ecclesiastical Council?

A. It is an assembly of the prelates of the Church,
convoked by their legitimate head, in order to decide

questions which may arise concerning the truths of religion, and to reform the morals of the Christian people, and ecclesiastical discipline. A Council is not always assembled for all these motives at once ; it may be convened for one or other of them.

How many kinds of Councils are there?

A. There are four kinds, viz.: a General Council, to which all the Bishops of the Catholic world are summoned by the Sovereign Pontiff. It is not necessary, however, that all should assist at it. A National Council, to which all the Bishops of a nation or kingdom are summoned by the Primate. A Provincial Council, to which the Metropolitan summons all the Bishops of the province who are his suffragans, and even such as are exempt, according to the terms of the Council of Trent. A Diocesan Council, to which the Bishop summons those priests of the diocese who have cure of souls, or an ecclesiastical benefice.

Has the Roman Pontiff alone the right to convoke a General Council?

A. All Catholics agree that this right belongs solely to the Roman Pontiff. Heretics pretend that this right 'belongs to the Emperor; but this pretence is most foolish, since it would be necessary that all the kingdoms of the world should be subject to the Emperor, if he is to exercise in them an act of jurisdiction, by convocation of the bishops. Moreover, he must hold the primacy in the Church, if the Bishops are to be obliged to assemble at his order.

The Roman Pontiff alone has supreme power and jurisdiction over all the Christians of the world, and therefore over all Bishops. You must observe that if Councils have sometimes been convoked by the Roman Emperor, it was done with the consent, and by order of the Roman Pontiff. All sound theologians and historians are agreed on this point.

To whom does it belong to preside at a General Council?

A. To the Roman Pontiff, as it belongs to the head to preside over the members. He may preside, however, either in person, or by means of his legates. This is the doctrine of all Catholic theologians.

What prelates may assist at a General Council?

A. Of ordinary right, Bishops alone can assist and give decisive votes, as judges of religious controversies. Cardinals, who are not also Bishops assist, and give their votes, as advisers of the Sovereign Pontiff; as also Abbots and Generals of religious orders, by privilege. Temporal sovereigns, or their ambassadors, assist as protectors.

Is a General Council of infallible authority?

A. No Catholic has ever doubted that it is of infallible authority; it has not, however, such authority, until after the approbation and confirmation of the Roman Pontiff.

Are other Councils, which are not General Councils, infallible?

A. Of themselves they are only authoritative

and not infallible; for infallibility is promised only to the Universal Church, and to him who represents it. We say, of themselves, because whenever their decisions have been approved by the Roman Church, they become infallible. Further, you must observe that, in matters regarding discipline, they are of obligation only for the places in which they are made; that is, if they are national, for that nation; if they are provincial, for that province; if diocesan, for that diocese.

SECT. V. *The Roman Pontiff.*

Who is the Roman Pontiff?

A. The Roman Pontiff is the Bishop who is the successor of St. Peter in the Roman See.

Has the Roman Pontiff all the privileges of St. Peter, and all the authority which he had over the Church?

A. He has all the privileges and all the authority which St. Peter received from Christ, when He constituted him Head of the Apostolic College, and of His Church; that is to say, he has the same jurisdiction and authority over all the Bishops, and over all the faithful. This is of faith.

Is it then an article of the Faith that the Roman Pontiff has the primacy over all the Church?

A. It is an article of the Faith, specially defined in the Council of Florence, with the full consent of both Greeks and Latins.

Is this primacy of the Roman Pontiff in the Church necessary?

A. A society that had many independent heads, such as Bishops would be without the Roman Pontiff, could not but result in confusion and anarchy. The very heretics themselves acknowledge this, when they give jurisdiction to the Emperor, or to Kings over Bishops.

Supposing it were at any time necessary to call the Roman Pontiff to account for disorderly or wicked conduct, to whom would belong the right of judging his case?

A. God has reserved this right to Himself. No one on earth can judge the Roman Pontiff. Besides the authorities which might be adduced, a palpable reason is this:—The head of a government can never be called to account, save in case of a revolt; but the Church does not admit revolt within her bosom. If a revolt occur in the Church, from the mere fact that it is a revolt, those who promote it, and those who take part in it, are separated and cut off from the Church, at least as schismatics; and therefore, as separated from her, they no longer have any authority in her. The Roman Pontiff may be fraternally admonished, but not judged.

When the Roman Pontiff, as Head and Master of the whole Church, decides a controversy in matters of faith and morals, or, to use theological terms, when he defines *ex cathedra*, is he infallible in his judgment?

A. He is infallible, as might be proved by every sort of authority and reason. It is an established fact, that when the Roman Pontiffs have defined any question, in their quality of Heads and Masters of the Church, they have never erred. Contumacious men have ever been found to reclaim against the truth of the Pontifical decisions, but the matter has always ended by the whole Church accepting the Pontifical decisions, and declaring the recusants to have fallen into heresy.*

Is the authority of the Roman Pontiff inferior to the authority of a General Council ?

A. The Roman Pontiff, by his authority, gives force to a General Council, and therefore he is superior, and not inferior to it. The Supreme Pontiff does not cease to be Head of the Church when the Church is assembled in Council. Remember

---

* The Nestorians and Eutychians opposed the decisions of St. Leo the Great ; the Monothelites, those of St. Martin I. ; the Lutherans, those of Leo X.; the Jansenists, those of Innocent X., Alexander VII., &c. But these and all others, both ancient and modern, who have imitated them in their opposition to the decisions of the Roman Pontiffs, are all heretics in the judgment of Catholics. The condemnations of the Roman Pontiffs are called, and are, thunderbolts which issue from the Throne of God, and there is no shield which they will not shiver in pieces. There is no escape for him who provokes them, unless he submits, and humbly pronounces his own condemnation. It is impossible to repel them. They are like the arrow of Jonathan, of which Holy Scripture says :—" The arrow of Jonathan never turned back." (2 Kings, i. 22.)

that no General Council has ever been recognised as infallible by the Church, without the confirmation and approbation of the Pope. Remember, moreover, that it is impossible to conceive the idea of a General Council without the Pope. The Pope must convoke it, must preside over it, either in person or by his legates, and finally, as we have said, must confirm it. To conceive a General Council without the Pope, we must conceive a General Council in opposition to the Pope; and in that case it would be an unlawful material assembly of Bishops, all really disunited, because without a centre of unity.

This would be the case in regard to a Pope living at the time a General Council was assembled; but would the Pope be subject to the decrees of former General Councils, lawfully celebrated, and confirmed by the authority of the Popes his predecessors?

A. Undoubtedly, in dogmatic decisions, because that which was true, and infallibly true once, will be true to all eternity: moreover, to say that the Pope must in this way be subject to Councils, is the same as to say that the Pope must be catholic; which no one doubts. In decisions, however, which regard discipline, which in the Church is changeable, the Pope is superior to Councils, and may derogate from their laws when he sees necessity for so doing; and this authority is necessary to him, for otherwise the well-being of the Church would be ill-provided for.

Why would the well-being of the Church be ill-provided for?

A. For this reason; as an inferior can in no case derogate from the laws of a superior, so the Pope would be unable in any case to dispense or derogate from the canons of Councils; therefore for every dispensation and for every derogation, which a council had not authorized the Supreme Pontiff or others to make, it would be necessary to convoke a General Council. Now we all know how difficult a matter this is, and that many times it would even be an impossibility. Hence on many occasions the Church would lack the means of providing for her own needs.*

* The Infallibility of the Supreme Pontiff in his dogmatic decisions, and his authority over General Councils, are now dogmas, not only Divinely revealed, but proposed by the Church, and so binding on the intellects and consciences of all the faithful, under pain, not only of error, but of heresy. *See the definition on this point, of the Vatican Council, Note, page* 27. This Council also teaches and declares—"that the Roman Pontiff is the Supreme Judge of the faithful; and that, in all causes pertaining to ecclesiastical examination, recourse may be had to his judgment; and that the judgment of the Apostolic See, than whose authority there is no greater, can be revised by no man; and that to no one is it lawful to judge its judgment, and that they therefore err from the right way of truth, who affirm that it is lawful to appeal from the judgment of the Roman Pontiff to an Œcumenical Council, as to an authority superior to the Roman Pontiff." Chap. iv.

The authorities quoted in the text will serve to shew the previous absolute theological certainty of the doctrine, which is now also of Catholic faith.—ED.

However it is not a truth defined, as of faith that the Pope is infallible in his dogmatic decisions, and that he has authority over General Councils.*

A. It is true that this is not in the number of those truths which must be firmly believed, under pain of heresy in him who does not believe them. Still it is one of the most certain truths which we have in theology next to the dogmas which are of faith. The following proposition was condemned by Alexander VIII., the 7th December, 1690. "The assertion of the authority of the Roman Pontiff over an Œcumenical Council, and his infallibility in determining questions of faith, is futile, and has repeatedly been overthrown." He who should defend such a proposition would incur an excommunication reserved to the Pope.

Has the Pope authority to declare books to be heretical or scandalous, and to prohibit such?

A. Undoubtedly he has, for as Universal Pastor it is for him to determine what pastures are unwholesome, and to hinder his flock from approaching them.

When the Pope declares that a book contains a certain heresy, must we blindly submit our own judgment to his declaration?

A. There is no room to doubt it; because in matters of faith the homage of the tongue which submits to keep silence is not sufficient, there is required also the submission of the heart, that is

---

* This Divine truth is now of Catholic faith, as defined by the Vatican Council. See notes on pages 27 and 39.—ED.

to say, of the will, which is made with submission of the understanding. This truth, which was always recognized in the Church, has in these later times been more clearly illustrated by the fact of the condemnation of the heretical propositions of Jansenius.

SECT. VI. *The Holy Fathers, the Doctors and the Schoolmen.*

Who are the Holy Fathers?

A. The Holy Fathers are those great men, who, for their great learning, sanctity, and antiquity have, either expressly or tacitly, been declared such by the Church. The last of the Holy Fathers was St. Bernard.

Who are the Doctors?

A. Men famous for learning and sanctity, declared such by the Church, as St. Thomas, St. Bonaventure, &c.

When the Holy Fathers and the Doctors of the Church are unanimous in affirming anything pertaining to faith and morals, may we doubt of its truth?

A. We may not doubt of it, for they are the depositaries of the Tradition of the Church, and if they are unanimous in affirming any truth in such matters, it is as much as to say that it comes directly from the Apostles.

Is it necessary that they be all agreed, without any exception?

A. This is not necessary, for no one of the Holy Fathers, of himself alone, is infallible, and any one of them might be mistaken, and so not agree with the rest : in such case the error of one must not detract from the force of the truth taught by all, or nearly all.

The opinion of one Holy Father must then be accounted of no weight ?

A. Not so ; on the contrary it must be accounted of great weight, if it be not opposed to the common opinion of the other Fathers ; if however it be contrary to their judgment, it must not be regarded.

Who are the Schoolmen ?

A. Those who wrote after the Doctors of the Church, in defence of truths contradicted by heretics. They were very numerous in the sixteenth century, and opposed the heretics of that age ; for this reason the Schoolmen are hated and abused by all Protestants even in these days, as well as by persons of doubtful or insincere belief, although they may affect Catholicism and union with Holy Church.

What authority have the Schoolmen ?

A. If all are commonly agreed in affirming anything appertaining to faith and morals, their authority is irrefragable, even before such truth is expressly defined by the Church; for we cannot suppose that all the learned men who adorn the Church should be mistaken; or that, if they were mistaken, the Church would not condemn their error, but suffer it to be thus authorized, and taught by all. If, however, they are not generally agreed, but are divided in their opinions, each one has no further authority than the weight of the reasons which he adduces. This is meant however, speaking generally; for the Schoolmen, who have been specially distinguished for right judgment and profound knowledge of the Holy Fathers, have a personal authority of great account. Who, for example, would not shew consideration for the opinion of Bellarmine, if it were only because he was so judicious, and learned in ecclesiastical science?* However, the authority of the Schoolmen can never be put on a par with that of the Holy Fathers or of the Doctors.

SECT. VII.*History, Human Reason, and Philosophy.*

What authority has History?

A. History has considerable authority in religious controversies, for it furnishes great light, and supplies many facts for the elucidating, and proving of truth, and for the confutation of error. Nevertheless he who would sincerely make use of the authority of History in matters of religion, must not be content with a mere superficial knowledge, nor with the knowledge of disconnected and isolated facts, for if

---

* When his Holiness, Clement VIII., elected Bellarmine Cardinal, he said of him to the Sacred College, "We have chosen this man, because the Church of God has not his equal as to doctrine!"

in regard to all sciences, it is better to be ignorant of them, than to have an incorrect knowledge of them, this is especially true in regard to History. I speak of Ecclesiastical History, as being the most necessary for theological controversies; profane history, generally, cannot be so useful.

What authority have Human Reason and Philosophy?

A. They have considerable authority, when they are held subject to Faith, and are used in such theological controversies as admit of the arguments which they furnish. You may easily imagine that if the Faith were subject to Reason and to Philosophy, the Faith would be destroyed. They cannot decide in matters which are in no way within their sphere. How, for instance, could the existence of the mystery of the Most Holy Trinity be proved from Philosophy?

CHAPTER II.

GOD—THE ONE AND TRINE?

Who is God?

A. He is a Lord infinitely perfect, the Creator and Preserver of heaven and earth, and of all things visible and invisible.

What do those words *infinitely perfect*, signify?

A. They mean that in God is all good, and that He is Infinite Goodness.

What does the word *infinite* signify?

A. It signifies something that has no end. For example, if there were a sea whose bottom we could never fathom, how deep soever we might dive, whose surface we could never reach, how high soever we might soar, whose shores we could never find, though we might continually pass from side to side ; or better still, if there were a bottomless, surfaceless, shoreless sea, and if this sea spread itself on all sides without limit, this would be an infinite sea. Observe, however, that it is impossible that any *material* thing, such as the sea is, for example, could be infinite.

But supposing such a sea to exist, would it be a figure of the Goodness of God?

A. Yes. The Goodness of God is as great spiritually, as this huge sea would be materially, were its existence possible. The Goodness of God has no limit or term ; no one can measure it ; no one, not even the Angels, can comprehend it ; God alone, by His infinite Wisdom, comprehends His own infinite Goodness.

Could we find no creature, either in heaven or on earth, whose goodness might be put in comparison with the Goodness of God?

A. As there can be no comparison between time and eternity, so there can be no comparison between the goodness of any creature whatsoever, and the Goodness of God. The ineffable goodness of even the Ever Blessed Virgin is not only little, but we might even say, is nothing, compared with the infinite Goodness of God. Hence it is that not even in Paradise, can the Angels, the Saints, or the Most Blessed Virgin herself—with all the immense love which they bear to God—approach to loving Him as much as He merits to be loved in Himself. God alone loves Himself, as much as He merits to be loved.

What is meant by this Infinite Goodness?

A. The aggregate, the union of His infinite Perfections or Attributes; His Omnipotence by which He can make or destroy all things, by an act of His Will; His Wisdom, by which He clearly sees the past, the present, the future, and all possible things; His Justice, with which he rewards the good, and chastises the wicked; His Mercy, with which He pardons the sins of those who with a true heart repent; His Eternity, whereby He has never had any beginning, and whereby likewise He shall have no end; His Immensity, by which

He is in Heaven, on earth, and in every place; His
Impassibility, by which He Who is a most pure
and perfect Spirit, cannot suffer or endure any evil
whatsoever; and all His other infinite perfections
by which He is truly an Infinite Good.

What do you mean by saying that God is a *most
pure Spirit?*

A. I mean that God has not a body as we have,
therefore we cannot picture Him to ourselves as
high or low, or broad or narrow; we cannot touch
Him with our hands, nor can we see Him with the
material eyes of our body.

Then He is nothing?

A. On the contrary, you should say that He is
all things, because He is infinitely rich in every
perfection, and in all good. He is not material,
such as are the things we see and touch, and
therefore He has not the properties of material
things, which are large or small, broad or narrow
and which may be seen and touched; but He has
all spiritual perfections, by which He is a spirit
infinitely good. Our soul is also a spirit which can
neither be seen nor touched, and yet our soul thinks,
judges, reasons, gives motion to the whole body,
and is a far more noble part of man than his body.

How can you say that God has no body, when
Holy Scripture speaks of the eyes of God, the ears
of God, the hands of God, and of other members
of His body?

A. When Holy Scripture attributes to God

members of the human body, it does so in a figurative sense. If I say that a horse flies rapidly over the plain, I do not mean that the horse has wings and flies like a bird: by the word *fly* I intend to signify the speed with which he traverses the country, so, when Holy Scripture speaks of the eyes and ears of God, it means to signify His Wisdom, whereby He sees and knows all things; when it speaks of His hands it means to signify His Omnipotence, whereby He performs all His works; and so as to the rest. All Theologians and interpreters resolve such difficulties in this way. In fact when Scripture speaks literally, it says, God is a Spirit (John iv. 24); and this is an article of the Faith.

Why do you say that God is a *most simple Spirit* ?

A. Because there is no composition of diverse substances in God, nor any real distinction of perfections or attributes. The Omnipotence of God is God Himself. The Wisdom of God is God Himself; and so we may say of His Justice, of His Mercy, and of all His other perfections. In man, power, wisdom, and piety, are things distinct from the man himself, and therefore a man may exist without power, without wisdom, and without piety. But in God every attribute is God Himself, neither more nor less. Thus do all theologians, with St. Bernard, answer those heretics who have imagined that in God there is real distinction between His Attributes.

Why then do you say that God has so many attributes, and so many diverse perfections?

A. We say so according to our mode of understanding, because the Divine Nature or Substance is omnipotent, wise, just, merciful, &c., although this omnipotence, wisdom, justice, &c., are in reality nothing else than the most simple Divine Substance itself.

Seeing that God is infinitely Good, and the Author of all things that exist, who produced evil in the world?

A. Evil came into the world, from the abuse of their liberty, in creatures gifted with free will. God has given this liberty to angels, and to men. The abuse which many of the Angels made of their liberty, when they sinned by pride, is the origin of all the evils which the devils suffer, and which they produce by their malice. The abuse which man made of his liberty is the origin of all the evils suffered by men. Observe, however, that the Holy Angels who remained faithful to God, cannot now any longer sin, that is, abuse their liberty.

Still there are so many evils in the world, which have not been produced by the abuse of liberty in the creature. For instance, Hell is a great evil, so are hurtful beasts, pestilence, earthquakes, &c. Is God the author of all these evils?

A. All those things, and others like them, are not evils in themselves. They are evils only to those who suffer them, inasmuch as they are afflicted by

4

them : in themselves they are benefits necessary to
hinder sin, and for the punishment of sin; they
manifest the Divine Justice, give occasion for the
exercise of virtue, &c. They are benefits, because
they are ordained by God against the one only true
evil, which is sin—that is, against the abuse of
liberty. If there were no sin in the world, there
would be no afflictions in it, that is, no punishment
for sin ; in like manner as if there were no criminals
in a kingdom, there would be no need of prisons,
or of other punishments.

But if God is infinitely 'good, why has He permitted His creatures to abuse their liberty and commit sin, the cause of so great miseries ?

A. God has given His creatures liberty, in order
that they may merit by making a good use of it, and
He gives them, at the same time, the necessary aid
that they may use it as He requires ; and more we
cannot expect from His infinite goodness. Further,
He brings forth greater good from the evils that are
committed : as, for example, when He has permitted
the cruelty of tyrants, in order to exercise the faith
and love of innumerable martyrs.

Some have imagined that we ought to recognize
two principles,—one of good, who would therefore be the good God, and another of evil, who
would therefore be the wicked God. They attributed all the good in the world to the first, and all
the evil to the second. Is not this opinion
plausible ?

A. This is not an opinion, but a most stupid heresy; for evil is not a reality. Evil is an imperfection, a lack of good, just as darkness is not a reality, but simply lack of light. Hence, a wicked God would be an infinite lack of good, and therefore an infinite nothing. Such an idea is contradictory, and a ridiculous imagination.

SECT. II. *The Immensity and Providence of God.*

How are we to understand that God is Immense ?

A. God is Immense, because He is not contained in any place, but, on the contrary, contains all places and the universe itself. He is everywhere by His Presence, clearly beholding all things; by his Power, preserving the existence of all creatures, and concurring to all their operations; by His Essence, because, as we have already said, the Wisdom and the Power of God are none other than the Divine Substance itself.

If God concurs to all the operations of creatures, do you mean to say that He concurs also to sin, and that therefore He approves it, and co-operates with it ?

A. In all free actions there is the *material* act and the *formal* of the act. In a murder the material act is the thrusting a dagger into a body, which, of itself, is an indifferent action ; the *formal* of the act is the evil will, that is, the wickedness of unjustly depriving a man of life. Now God concurs to the material act, inasmuch as it is an indifferent action, but

4—2

He does not concur to the *formal* of the act, that is, to the wickedness; on the contrary, He disapproves, condemns, and punishes it.

What is the Providence of God?

A. It is the disposition of all created things, in order to the attainment of their last end.

Does God exercise His providence towards all his creatures, without exception?

A. This is of faith: "He has equally care of all," as we read in the book of Wisdom, vi. 8.

Many things in the world happen by chance, which would not be the case if the Divine Providence regulated all things.

A. I will shew you your error by a comparison of St. Thomas. A master sends one of his servants to the market place. Unknown to him, he sends another to the same place, without telling him that he has already sent the first, because he desires that they should both meet there unexpectedly. The two servants, at first meeting one another, would think they had met by chance, while, in fact, their meeting is of premeditated design. You will understand from this that nothing in the world happens by chance. Our ignorance, through which we know not the causes of many things, has made us imagine that they happen by chance; but, instead of this, God rules all things by His providence, and nothing happens without a reason determined by Him. For instance, a leaf falls from a tree: why should it lie straight on the earth rather than the reverse ? It is impossible for us to know the reason; but there is a reason for it in the Divine Providence. Chance and fortune are mere names without reality, nor can they signify aught save our ignorance of the causes of things.

Does the Providence of God extend to all the free actions of men, both good and bad?

A. Undoubtedly : directing, moreover, the evil actions to some good. The sons of Jacob sold Joseph, because of the envy they cherished against him. God directed and overruled this barbarous sale in order to the advantage of the Egyptians, to the salutary confusion of his envious brethren, to the preservation and glory of the family of Jacob, &c.

You mean to say that God is the First Cause of all things : but are there not second causes, on which all things in their events depend?

A. There are indeed second causes; because, for example, it is water that wets us, it is fire that burns us: but still, you must observe that all second causes act in dependence on the First Cause, so that, whatever happens, always excepting the malice of sin, we must recognize as coming from God. Observe, also, that God does not always make use of secondary causes, for He can act without them. If it be His will to send a pestilence or an earthquake, He can make use of secondary causes, but he can also act immediately by Himself, without availing Himself of them, that is, without permitting the gene-

rating of the poisonous insects which naturally produce pestilence, and without permitting the rarefac-
tion and condensation of subterranean vapours, or
that disturbance of the equilibrium of electricity
which in the ordinary way occasions earthquakes ;
but observe carefully, that this is a matter of as
much indifference as it would be a matter of indifference whether the king punished a criminal absolutely, by a sentence written with his own hand, or
by a sentence caused by him to emanate from his
tribunals. Attend especially to this truth, for it is
precisely in these days, by continually crying out in
all circumstances of public or private chastisements,
that they are the effect of secondary causes, that
men seek to extinguish and dissipate that salutary
fear of God which might correct sinners. Be it so,
that all is the effect of secondary causes ; it is God,
notwithstanding, who regulates those secondary
causes by His Providence. He is a king who does
not write the sentence with His own hand, but
causes it to emanate from His tribunals. He does
not execute it with His own hands, but causes it to
be executed by His ministers : all the same, the
sentence and the punishment come from the king.
Above all, therefore, remember, that to reward, to
punish, or to do any other act whatever, God has
no need of secondary causes ; and when He does
adopt them, it is always He who rewards, He who
punishes, and He who acts, by His Providence.

SECT. III. *The Will of God; Predestination and Reprobation.*

What is the Will of God?

A. The Will of God, which is one of His Attributes, which we conceive in God as, as it were, faculties, such as His Understanding and His Omnipotence; is that perfection by which He loves good and hates evil; that perfection by which He is directed in all His operations. Observe, that as there is no real distinction between the Perfections of God and God Himself, the Will of God is none other than the Divine Substance and Essence itself.

Is the Will of God free in its operations?

A. It is free—not to will evil, because God would not be Infinite Goodness if it were possible for Him to will the very least evil; but it is free in willing good, without being forced to do so by anything whatsoever. For example, God was free to create the world, and free not to create it; and this is the case in regard to all those other operations of His which are called operations *ad extra.*

Which are His operations *ad extra?*

A. They are the creation, preservation, and government of all things. They are called *ad extra,* to distinguish them from those which take place in God Himself, which are called *ad intra,* and in regard to which the Divine Will is not free, because they are *necessary* operations, essential to the Divine nature. As we have already said, God might or might not create the world, but the Father was not free not to generate the Son, that is to say, the Eternal Word ; nor the Holy Ghost free not to proceed from the Father and from the Son, because this generation and this procession are absolutely necessary in the Divine Substance, according to the idea which the Faith gives us of God.

Must we acknowledge Love in God ?

A. God loves Himself infinitely, and He also loves his creatures, particularly His intelligent and rational creatures, such as the angels and men.

Must we acknowledge hatred in God?

A. God hates sin and sinners. He does not, however, hate sinners in that they are His creatures, but in that they are sinners : when they cease from sin, He no longer hates them.

I wish to know if God wills the eternal salvation of all men.

A. God sincerely wills the eternal salvation of all men. This was always the faith of all Catholics in all ages, according to the sense of Holy Scripture, and the tradition of all the Fathers. The contrary error, which is, that God wills only the salvation of some men, was solemnly condemned in Calvin, and afterwards in Jansenius.

I can easily understand that God wills the salvation of all the faithful, because He furnishes them with the means necessary to obtain it ; but how can you say that He wills the salvation of infidels who have no means whatever of gaining it ?

A. It is false that infidels have no means whatever of obtaining eternal salvation; God gives many graces to infidels, and if they did not abuse them, He would bring them to the knowledge of the true faith, that so they might be saved; and He would do this, even if it required miracles, as St. Thomas teaches.

At least you must admit that God does not will the salvation of children, who die without Baptism, and particularly of those who die before coming to the light?

A. Holy Scripture, the Fathers, and the sentiment of the whole Church give us sufficient assurance that God wills the salvation of every soul, and therefore also of the souls of such children; nor must we say the contrary, though it may be difficult for us to understand in what manner He wills it. In our Holy Religion it is not only what we can understand that is true; we must believe many things without understanding them, and this is one.

What do you say in regard to the Predestination and Reprobation of men?

A. It is an article of the Faith that there is true Predestination, that is to say, that from all eternity God has determined to give Paradise to some men; and that there is true Reprobation, that is to say, that from all eternity God has decreed to condemn some men to Hell; and hence the number of both the one and the other is determined. The predestinate are all those who die in the grace of God, the reprobate are all those who die in mortal sin.

These answers seem to me too material, could you not speak more profoundly of such mysteries?

A. It is enough for me to explain to you what is most necessary to be known: many things which might be added are not necessary for all, nor suited to all. In regard to predestination and reprobation it is sufficient for you to know, that God sincerely wills the eternal salvation of all men; and sincerely willing it, He grants to all means sufficient to obtain it. (When I say sufficient, I understand means, which really suffice, because, if in fact they did not suffice, they would not be sufficient means). These means are His graces, without which we cannot obtain salvation; those who correspond to this grace will certainly be saved, and therefore are predestinate. Observe that it is St. Peter (2 Ep. St. Peter, i. 10) who exhorts you to make sure your election to eternal life by means of your good works, and it will be well if the simple Divine Word content you, without seeking further. Moreover the reprobate must not be looked upon as persons to whom God on His part, has been wanting, but as persons who merit to be excluded from the Kingdom of God for their wickedness.

What do you say about children who die before the use of reason, some baptized and some not, and so, some predestinate and others reprobate?

A. Children who are predestinate are so through the merits of Jesus Christ, applied to them by means of Holy Baptism. That such a lot is theirs, is the work of Divine Mercy. Children who are reprobate, are such through original sin, by which they die deprived of sanctifying grace. That such a misfortune should be theirs is an act of Divine Justice. But you who read this ought not to penetrate too far into these mysteries; if they present difficulties which the Holy Fathers could not solve, how much greater must these difficulties be to you? Do you suppose that by force of reasoning you would ever come to know the secrets of an earthly sovereign, if he did not choose to manifest them to you? Certainly not. How much less then can you come to know the secrets of the King of Heaven if He will not discover them to you.* We find mysteries in the conduct of finite men, which we cannot solve, and shall we wonder because we find them in the dispositions of Infinite Divine Wisdom? In whatever way God may predestinate the good, or reprobate the wicked, it is impossible but that His purpose should be most just, and worthy of His Infinite Goodness. Let it suffice for you to know that God loves you more than you love yourself; that God wills your salvation more than you desire it yourself; that God will not exclude you from His Kingdom unless

* " To will not to know what the best of masters wills not to teach, is a wise ignorance."—Scaliger.

you refuse it of your own free will. He has already done more for us,—redeeming us at so much cost, and calling us into the bosom of His Church; now there remains but the lesser work, which is to give us fitting aids in order that we may profit by His Infinite mercies, and this He will do; have this hope and you will not be confounded.

There is yet another difficulty which I cannot pass over in silence. It is impossible that what God has appointed should not come to pass; therefore, if God have predestinated Titius to glory it is impossible that Titius should be damned; while if He have reprobated Caius, it is impossible that Caius should be saved.

A. To avoid perplexing ourselves, we must first of all consider, that God never works but by the rules of an Infinite Wisdom; therefore, although we may not know it, there must always be a most just reason for His predestinating Titius and not Caius.* Besides he predestinates Titius, who will

---

* "He has not mercy on those to whom, by an equity most hidden, and far removed from human perceptions, He judges that grace is not to be afforded. This the Apostle does not disclose, but marvels at, saying, 'O the height of the riches of God.'"—*Saint Augustine.* The same Holy Father affirms (Enchir. q. 95) that in Paradise we shall see such reasons and such causes as are now hidden from us; and similarly we shall know for what motive God has conferred many of His graces on those whom He foresaw would not profit by them, and has not conferred them on those who would have derived profit from them. St. Bonaventure

freely do good, by means of which he will merit glory, and He rejects Caius, who will freely do evil, by means of which he will merit damnation, so that we cannot say that Titius will necessarily be saved, and Caius necessarily damned.

But since God foresees that Titius will do good and that Caius will do evil, and since the Divine Foreknowledge cannot be mistaken, must not this good and this evil be done of necessity? If then God sees that I am in the number of the predestinate it is impossible that I should be damned; if, on the contrary He sees that I am in the number of the reprobate, it is impossible that I should be saved.

A. You must reflect that God's Prevision is none other than His Infinite Knowledge, to which the past and the future is always present. It is a simple vision of things, which does not deprive free causes of their liberty. For instance, I see one man steal, and I see another man give alms; when I see the former stealing, I do not say that, because I see him, he steals of necessity, but that he is certainly stealing; when I see the latter giving alms, I do not say that, because I see him, he does so of necessity, but that he is certainly doing so;

---

teaches the same doctrine. Observe, however, that such causes, reasons, and motives, cannot be other than most worthy of God, that is to say, of Infinite Goodness. Our ignorance should humble us, but not discourage us.

therefore God, when He foresees our future actions, does not necessitate them. This is the teaching of all true philosophers, along with all theologians, and so, God's seeing you in the number of the predestinate, or of the reprobate, is but His seeing the good or the bad use which you make of your liberty. Hence you may know that this difficulty, which appears to you so serious, means no more than this: if you, dying well, merit Paradise, it is impossible that you be damned; if, on the contrary, dying ill, you merit Hell, it is impossible that you be saved. So that, notwithstanding the dogma of Predestination and Reprobation, that which the Holy Ghost declares will always come to pass, namely, that life and death is in the hand of man (Eccles. xv. 18), and that it depends on man himself whether he will be saved or damned.

Then we may not say that God, as absolute master of His creatures, without having regard to future merits or demerits, elects some men for Paradise and destines others to Hell?

A. So Calvin blasphemously maintained. God, it is true can predestinate men to Paradise, and give them all opportune and efficacious aids, in order that they may attain it, although they have no right to such predestination; but He cannot destine His creatures to eternal misery, without foreseeing their demerits. The reason is, that the liberality which confers gifts on those who have no right to pretend to them, is a perfection, and therefore is in God; on the contrary, the cruelty and injustice, which would destine men to punishment without pre-supposing sin in them, are repulsive vices which destroy the idea, not only of infinite, but even of ordinary goodness.

SECT. IV. *The Beatific Vision.*

Do the Saints in Heaven see God?

A. They see Him intuitively, that is to say, they see Him in Himself, really as He is.

Does not Holy Scripture say that God is Invisible, and that no one has ever seen Him?

A. It says that God is Invisible, and that no one ever saw Him in this life. On this account the most probable opinion among the interpreters of Scripture is, that not even Moses saw Him intuitively; but that it was an Angel who appeared to him, and gave him orders and commands in God's name; they assert therefore that, when he says that he saw God, he means to say that he saw an Angel who spoke to him in the person of God. But it is a truth of the faith, that in the other life we shall see God, and we shall "see Him as He is," according to the expression of Scripture (1 John iii. 2).

After the Resurrection, shall we see God with the eyes of our body?

A. We shall never see God with our bodily eyes, because God is a pure Spirit. Our bodily eyes are material, and will be material, even after our Resurrection; and it is certain that material eyes cannot see spiritual things. But we shall see God with our intellect, illuminated by the Light of Glory.

What is this Light of Glory?

A. It is a supernatural habit, by which the mind, whether of men or Angels, is perfectly disposed to see God.

Could we not see God, even in Heaven, without this Light of Glory?

A. It is certain that we could not see Him, any more than, with our bodily eyes however strong, we could see a mountain, however near it might be to us, without the aid of light.

What shall we see in God?

A. We shall see His Divine Substance with His Divine Perfections, which are in reality but the same most simple Divine Substance, (as we have already shewn in the 1st Section, answer to the 10th question); the mystery of the most Holy Trinity; and we shall also see creatures, as effects in their cause.

I wish to know whether, when we see God clearly in Heaven, we shall comprehend Him?

A. To comprehend God, it is not sufficient to see God clearly. To comprehend Him it would be necessary to know Him with that perfection wherewith God, by his Infinite Knowledge, knows Himself; and this is impossible for any creature. And so, not even the most Holy Soul of Jesus Christ, which is hypostatically united to His

Divinity, can arrive at comprehending God, that is to say, knowing Him, with that perfection with which God knows Himself.

In Heaven shall we understand all the mysteries of the Faith, which now we must blindly believe?

A. No one has ever doubted that in Heaven is seen clearly all that we believe on earth; and so the Saints in Heaven have not the virtue of Faith, whereby we believe what we do not see.

Will all the Saints in Heaven see God equally?

A. It is an article of the Faith that the Beatific Vision in Heaven will not be alike for all, but proportioned to the greater or less merits of each. (So the Councils of Florence and Trent.) This diversity arises from the greater or less Light of Glory which the Saints will enjoy, and which is measured by the greater or less charity with which they will be inflamed in Heaven.

Will not such diversity be displeasing to the Saints?

A. They are no longer capable of envy; but rejoice in the good of others as in their own, and the felicity of those who are among the least in the Kingdom of Heaven is so great, and so commensurate to the capacity which they have for enjoyment, that there remains nothing for them to desire. The following comparison will explain the truth of this. A man and a child, both thirsty, reach the banks of a great river. The man drinks, and so does the

5

child. Do you suppose that the child, who must needs drink less on account of the capacity of his stomach, envies the greater quantity which the man drinks? The child is content with being able to drink as much as he wants, and as much as he can.

Are we to believe that God grants the Vision of Himself, to the Holy Souls in Paradise, before the Resurrection of the Body, and the General Judgment?

A. It is an article of the Faith, as appears from the definition of Faith of the Council of Florence, 25th Sept., that souls, fully purged from all sin, and released from all punishment due to sin, are admitted at once to the clear Vision of God in Paradise.

What is to be said in regard to the opinion which teaches, that after the Resurrection, the Saints, together with Christ, will reign here upon earth for a thousand years?

A. This is a heresy of the Apollinarians, condemned by the first Council of Constantinople. The reign of the Blessed and of Christ will be in Heaven, and not upon earth, and it will be eternal.

SECT. V.—*The Mystery of the Most Holy Trinity.*

I wish that in speaking to me of this Mystery, so sublime and difficult, you would use the strictest terms of the Schools, in order to my more certain and exact understanding of it.

A. I intend so to speak to you of this mystery that every word may be available for teaching the

Catechism to children, therefore it is not my intention to make rigorous use of the terms of the Schools, which would not be understood, and would require too prolix explanations. You must be content that I explain such things as are most necessary for you to know, with the utmost brevity, and in the clearest and most intelligible terms.

How do you define the Mystery of the most Holy Trinity?

A. One God subsisting in Three Persons.

! How is it possible that God, being one and most simple, subsists in Three Persons?

A. There are two truths, equally of faith;—that God is one and most simple in His Divine Substance, and trine in Persons, who are called the Father, the Son, and the Holy Ghost. This is a mystery however, which, while on earth, we must adore, and which we shall not understand, till we can contemplate it in Paradise.

It seems to me, however, to be a contradiction that he who is three should be one, or that he who is one should be three.

A. There is no contradiction in it, because these Three Divine Persons have one and the same Divine Nature and Substance. It would be a contradiction if They had three diverse substances, because three substances would be three Gods, and could not be one only God.

We may say then that the Father is God, that the Son is God, and that the Holy Ghost is God?

A. You not only may, but you must say so. It is an article of the Faith ; for the Father has the Divine Substance, the Son has the Divine Substance, the Holy Ghost has the Divine Substance, which is one only, and so there is one only God.

Is the Father Eternal, the Son Eternal, and the Holy Ghost Eternal ?

A. Most certainly : but they are not three Eternals, but one Eternal, because one only God.

Is the Father Almighty, the Son Almighty, and the Holy Ghost Almighty ?

A. Undoubtedly : but they are not three Almighties, but only one Almighty ; and so it is in regard to the other attributes of God, which are the same one and indivisible substance of God, as we have already said (Ch. II., § 1, A. x.). *(See also the Athanasian Creed).*

Have the Persons of the most Holy Trinity the same Perfections, the same Understanding, and the same Will ?

A. They have the same Wisdom and the same Goodness. They live with the same Life, know with the same Understanding, will with the same Will, and work with the same Power. The reason of this is always the same, that they have the same Divine Nature and Substance.

May we then say that the Person of the Father is the Person of the Son, and the Person of the Holy Ghost ?

A. You must not say so, for it is an article of the

Faith that They are Three Persons, really distinct (*Athanasian Creed*); and therefore the Person of the Father is not the Person of the Son, nor of the Holy Ghost; the Person of the Son is not the Person of the Father, nor of the Holy Ghost; the Person of the Holy Ghost is not the Person of the Father, nor of the Son. They are Three Persons really distinct one from another, although They have the same Substance.

Can we say that God is distinct in Three Persons?

A. The expression that God is distinct in Three Persons is condemned by the dogmatic Bull *Auctorem Fidei;* hence you must say that in God there are Three distinct Persons, and not that God is distinct in Three Persons.

May we not say, in any sense whatever, that there are Three Gods?

A. No, in no sense whatever; whoever should say so would be a heretic.

May we say that God is Father, Son and Holy Ghost?

A. You should say so, as appears from the definition of the 4th Lateran Council.*

Give me some comparison which may render this less obscure to me.

---

* "We believe and confess that there is one Supreme, Incomprehensible and Ineffable Reality, which is truly Father, Son and Holy Ghost, Three Persons together, and each of them distinct."

A. Picture to yourself three persons called Peter, Paul, and John, who, nevertheless, had one and the same soul, and one and the same body. We should call them three persons, because one would be Peter, the other Paul, and the third John; they would, however, be one man only, and not three men, not having three bodies or three souls, but only one body and one soul. This would be impossible amongst men, because man's substance is little and limited, and therefore cannot be one and the same in more than one person; but the Substance of God, that is the Divinity, is infinite, and therefore can be found, and in fact, is found, in several persons. The Substance, therefore, that is to say, the Divinity of the Father, is found also in the Son and in the Holy Ghost.

Why is the Father called the First Person of the Most Holy Trinity?

A. Because the Father is without a Principle; that is to say, He has not His origin from, nor is produced by any one; but He is the Principle from which the other Persons proceed, and by whom they are produced.

Why is He called the Father?

A. Because from all eternity He produces or generates a Person like to and equal with Himself, of the self-same Substance and Nature, that is to say, the Son.

Then if the Son proceeded from the Father, the Father was the first to exist?

A. I have told you that the Father generates the Son from all eternity ; therefore the Father, who was from all eternity, from all eternity generated the Son, and ever generates Him eternal as Himself.

Why is the Second Person called the Son, and how is He generated?

A. He is called the Son because He is generated by the Father ; and this generation is by way of understanding and knowledge. The Father, from all eternity contemplates in Himself His Infinite Perfections, and, like a most clear mirror, produces a living and most perfect Image of Himself, which has His same Divine Substance, and is called the Son, and also the Eternal Word of God.

Why is the Third Person called the Holy Ghost?

A. Because He proceeds from the Father and from the Son by way of will and love, and is, as it were, a Spiritual Breath; and because He is the Love of God, He is essentially Holy.

How are we to understand His proceeding from the Father and from the Son, by way of will and love?

A. The Father and the Son, loving one another perfectly from all eternity, produce the Holy Ghost, who is the Mutual Love of the Father and the Son, and has the same Divine Substance. Observe here, that it is an article of the Faith that the Father proceeds from none, that the Son proceeds from the Father, and that the Holy Ghost proceeds from the Father and the Son.

Then the Father is the greatest of the Persons of the Most Holy Trinity, the Son is less than the Father, and the Holy Ghost less than the Father and the Son?

A. Fix thoroughly in your mind what has been so often said, — that the Persons of the Most Holy Trinity have the same Divine Nature and Substance, and therefore are all three Equal, and equally Perfect. Among the Persons of the Most Holy Trinity there is neither greater nor less, but a perfect equality of Goodness and Perfection.

CHAPTER III.

GOD—THE CREATOR.

SECT. I. *The Creation of the World ;—in general.*

WHAT is the meaning of the word *create ?*

A. *To create* means to bring out of nothing ; so that when we say that God created the world, we mean to say that God, by His omnipotence, drew the world out of nothing. *Creating* differs from *making,* inasmuch as in making anything we use materials which already exist, whereas, in creating, *existence* itself is given to things.

What end did God propose to Himself in the Creation of the World ?

A. In the Creation of the World, Almighty God proposed to Himself two ends, one primary, the other secondary. The primary end was the manifestation of His own perfections ; the secondary end was the felicity of intelligent creatures, both men and angels.

Creatures, then, manifest the Infinite Perfections of God ?

A. It is evident that they manifest them, because from creatures we know the Creator, His Omnipotence, His Wisdom, &c. They manifest them, however, in a limited degree, because creatures, being circumscribed and finite, cannot manifest the Infinite Perfections of God in their real extent. Observe, that God could have created a world, which, considered in itself, would have been more perfect than that which He has created, that is to say, which would have manifested in a more sublime degree His Divine Perfections. Nevertheless, this world is perfect of its own kind, manifesting in the best mode the Divine Perfections, in the degree in which it has pleased the Infinite Wisdom of God to manifest them. The Wisdom of God requires that He should choose the means most fitted to the attainment of His end : His Omnipotence demands that He should be able to do always more than He has done.

God attains the primary end for which He created the world, which is the manifestation of His Infinite Perfections, in the exact degree which He has determined ; but He does not attain the secondary end, for many intelligent creatures are not happy—men, for instance, on this earth, and the damned and the demons in hell.

A. God has given to all His intelligent creatures the necessary means of happiness ; therefore, on His part, He has attained the end for which He created them, which was conditional—that is, the rendering those intelligent creatures happy, who should will to be happy by making a good use of their liberty. If many intelligent creatures are not happy, it is because, abusing their own liberty, they have refused the happiness offered them, and become unhappy by their own fault. When I give alms, my end is to relieve the misery of my indigent neighbours : on my part, I attain my end, which is conditional, to relieve him, if he wills to be relieved : it is the fault of the poor man himself, if, abusing the liberty he has to make use of my alms, he throws it away, and so remains unrelieved.

Sect. II.—*The Angels.*

How do you define the Angels?

A. They are created, spiritual, complete, and intelligent substances. They are called *created* substances, because in the creation of the world they were drawn out of nothing. They are called *spiritual*, because they have no bodies, not even a most subtle body of air or light, as some of the Ancients supposed. No Catholic can now have any doubt on this head, the 4th Lateran Council having expressly declared in favour of the entire spirituality of the Angels. They are called *complete*, as differing from the human soul, which is designed, not by itself alone, but in union with a body, to form a whole,—that is, the person of man. They are called *intelligent*, because they have great force and subtlety of understanding ; so that they are called simply—*Intelligences.*

What does the name Angel signify?

A. Angel means *messenger;* therefore, the name Angel is given to the Celestial Intelligences, not as the proper name of their nature, but as the proper name of their office, when they are sent by God to discharge some embassy, or to give some counsel.

Is it an article of the Faith that Angels exist?

A. Undoubtedly it is, as is apparent from innumerable passages of Holy Scripture, and from the Chapter *Firmiter*, of the 4th Lateran Council.

Is the nature of Angels superior to human nature?

A. It is superior, as appears from Scripture and the Holy Fathers.

Do the Angels know our thoughts, and the secrets of our hearts?

A. They conjecture them from signs and indications which we give, even without reflection; they have not, however, a certain knowledge of them. They have certain knowledge of them, when we will that they should know our thoughts and the secrets of our hearts; and also, when God, for His own ends, reveals these to them, even without our willing it.

How can you affirm that the Angels have not bodies, since they have often appeared in visible forms?

A. On such occasions they adapted to themselves a body which was not their own; they assumed it when needful, and laid it aside as soon as they had executed the commissions which God sent them to accomplish among men.

Have the Angels power over material things?

A. They have greater power over them than

men have ; with their most subtle intelligence and strength they can produce wonderful effects even in material things, such as no man is capable of. They can move the winds, cause storms, produce earthquakes and pestilences, and heal diseases, humanly speaking, incurable.

May we not believe that all these things proceed immediately from natural causes, as philosophers teach ?

A. We do not say that every wind that blows, that every storm that rages, and that every destroying pestilence, comes immediately from the action of some Angel ; such things happen ordinarily by the immediate concourse of natural causes, subject to the government of God, as we have already said (Chap. ii., Sect. 2, Providence) ; but philosophers will never be able to prove that at times Angels do not co-operate in such things. Moreover, it is apparent from many passages of Holy Scripture, from the tradition of the Holy Fathers, and from the sentiment of the entire Catholic Church that they do concur in them ; hence, sound philosophers do not refuse to attribute this power over material things to the Angels.

Were the Angels created in a state of grace ?

A. Certainly ; they did not however enjoy the Vision of God, and it was in their own power to preserve or to lose grace, according to the good or bad use they made of their liberty.

Did they all preserve themselves in a state of grace ?

A. Many preserved themselves in grace; but a great part speedily fell into the sin of pride, were excluded from the kingdom of God, and condemned to Hell. I say *speedily*, because when Adam sinned, the Angels had already sinned, and had been transformed into demons. Meanwhile, the good Angels who remained humble, were admitted to the clear Vision of God, and became impeccable.

Who was the chief of the bad Angels, whom we now call demons?

A. Lucifer: who in this way is the Chief or Prince of all the proud.

What punishments followed on the sin of the Angels?

A. Four: 1, blindness of mind in regard to *supernatural* things; for a great knowledge of natural things they retain; 2, obstinacy of the will in evil; 3, privation of Paradise; 4, and the torment of eternal fire.

Can the evil Angels induce us to evil?

A. They can tempt us in various ways, but they cannot do violence to our will.

Is it true that enchantments and sorcery can be wrought by the power of demons, and by their power over natural things?

A. It is most true, as appears from many passages of Holy Scripture, as many undeniable facts demonstrate, and as is manifest from the sentiment of the Church in all ages. It is rash and ridiculous to venture to deny such a truth, which, moreover, in our days is made even more manifest and palpable by the wonders of table turning and spirit rapping, and by magnetism, the abuse of which has been condemned by the Church in two decrees, emanating from the Supreme Holy Roman and Universal Inquisition, of the 28th July, 1847, and the 30th July, 1856. Hence we may consider it certain that the devil, by permission of Almighty God, has power in many ways over the persons of men, and over natural causes.

Are there any obsessed by evil spirits?

A. Although more than once impostors have pretended to be obsessed by evil spirits, it is most certain that, even after the death of Christ, persons have been obsessed by the devil; this has been proved by incontrovertible evidence, and cannot be denied without accusing the Catholic Church of prejudice and ignorance; for she uses exorcisms over obsessed persons, and confers an Ecclesiastical Order, and consecrates Ministers for this purpose.

Still in our days many doubt it.

A. St. Thomas, speaking of those who in his time doubted these things, feared not to assert that this doubt sprang from a principle of unbelief *

---

* "It proceeds from a root of unbelief or incredulity, that they believe that demons exist only in the estimation of the vulgar." Even Cudworth does not hesitate to assert, that only the impious, and men suspected of Atheism, doubt of such matters.

What forbids our saying the same of those who doubt them in our own days? We add, moreover, that such men are lacking in logic, in criticism, and in erudition.

How many orders of Angels are there?

A. There are nine, which constitute three Hierarchies or Choirs; the highest containing the Seraphim, the Cherubim, and the Thrones; the next, the Dominations, the Virtues, and the Powers; the last, the Principalities, the Archangels, and the Angels.

Does God destine the Angels to be the guardians of men?

A. It is a truth, clearly expressed in Holy Scripture, that men are guarded by the Angels; but we cannot say that it is absolutely of Faith that each individual has his Guardian Angel: such, however, is the sentiment of all the Holy Fathers, and of all the Faithful, in opposition to the heretic Calvin. Moreover, theologians agree that there are Angels deputed to be the guardians of the various kingdoms of the earth, and of the different Churches or Dioceses which constitute the Catholic Church. The Archangel St. Michael, who formerly was the Guardian Angel of the Synagogue, is now the Guardian of the Universal Church.

What is the office of the Angel Guardians in regard to the men confided to them by God?

A. They guard them from perils and imminent evils; they hinder the demons from injuring them, suggest holy thoughts, pray for them, and offer their prayers to God, console the souls in Purgatory, and when they are fully purged, conduct them to Paradise.

SECT. III. *Man.*

Of what does man consist ?

A. Of soul and body.

What are the principal properties of the soul of man ?

A. It is simple, it is free, and it is immortal.

What do you mean by man's soul being *simple ?*

A. The soul of man is a spirit, not composed of parts, and therefore like to the Angels. It is neither high nor low, neither broad nor narrow ; it has neither right nor left, it can neither be seen with the eyes of the body, nor touched with the hands ; it is in the body, and gives life to the body, but it has not any of the qualities which the body has.

What do you mean by the soul being *free ?*

A. The soul knows good and evil, and has the power of applying itself to the one or the other as it pleases. When it does good, it is in its power not to do it, and when it does evil, it is equally in its power not to do it.

What do you mean by its being *immortal ?*

A. Not only does the soul survive the death of the body, but uniting itself again to the body in the day of the General Resurrection, it will share with the body a life which shall never end ; eternally

6

happy or unhappy according to its merits or demerits, that is to say, according to the good or bad
use it shall have made of its liberty.

Could not God cause the death of the soul of
man ; that is to say, could He not reduce it to
nothing ?

A. He could do so of absolute power. Moreover,
should He for a single moment cease to preserve it,
it would be immediately reduced to nothing, as
would be the case with every other creature ; but
having decreed to preserve man's soul in life for ever,
and His decree being immutable, He cannot reduce
it to nothing.

Is it an article of the Faith that the body of man
will rise again after death, and that it will be united
anew to the soul ?

A. It is an article of the Faith, expressed in
the Creed.

Who was the first man created by God ?

A. Adam was the first man created by God. He
then took one of his ribs, and of it formed Eve,
who was the first woman.

Relying on the Chronology of Holy Scripture, we
reckon about six thousand years from Adam to us;
but many learned men, skilled in the antiquity of
monuments, are of opinion that some of these are
ten or twelve thousand years old. If this be true,
it is as much as to say that Adam was not the first
man created by God, but that other men existed
before him.

A. There is no occasion for me to point out to you that those learned men, whom you call skilled in the antiquity of monuments, are either* impostors or ignorant. It is sufficient for you to know that they attribute ten thousand years or more to certain ancient monuments, particularly Egyptian monuments, in order to bring into discredit the Sacred Scriptures, and so to shake the foundations of our most holy Religion. Adam was the first man created by God. He is as old as Heaven and Earth, within five days, having been created on the sixth day of creation ; and all the buildings or monuments which are in the world are less ancient than Adam.

Did God create Adam and Eve in a state of grace ?

* The Author here condemns those men only who endeavour to undermine the facts, and cast discredit on the truths of Divine Revelation, as contained in Holy Scripture and tradition, and as proposed by the Catholic Church, on the ground that they are in contradiction to the conclusions of modern philosophy and the progress of science,—as, for instance, the Pre-Adamites and Co-Adamites, who maintain that Adam was not the first man, and that the human race has not sprung from one man and one woman, created and made in the beginning, immediately by God Himself ; both of which are facts Divinely revealed, and so for which we have a certainty greater than that of all human science—an infallible and Divine certainty.

He does not condemn the opinion that the six days of Creation were—not so many natural days, but epochs, or periods of years.—ED.

A. When God created Adam and Eve, He adorned them with sanctifying grace.

In the estate of innocence in which they were, could it be said that this sanctifying grace was natural in them, that is to say, due to nature?

A. No; this grace was a supernatural and gratuitous gift in Adam and Eve, therefore not due to their nature; and this truth is apparent, especially from the condemnation of the xxii. xxiii. and lxxix. propositions of Baius, condemned by the Supreme Pontiffs, St. Pius V., Gregory XIII., and Urban VIII., as well as from the condemnation of the xxxiv. and xxxv. propositions of Quesnel, made by His Holiness Clement XI.

Were Adam and Eve created immortal?

A. Certainly; and if they had persevered in good, they would have passed to the possession of eternal glory without dying. Observe, however, that even this immortality and destination to the glory of Paradise were supernatural gifts.

If sanctifying grace, immortality, immunity from concupiscence, and destination to the glory of Paradise were supernatural gifts, it is as much as to say that God might have created man in the same state in which he is now born since the fall.

A. Certainly; sin always excepted, God might have created man in the state in which he is now born, without detracting from His justice or His goodness.

Were they perfectly happy in respect both of soul and body?

A. There is no doubt of it, because all misery began from sin; therefore, had they remained obedient in the terrestrial Paradise, where God placed them, they would never have suffered the least affliction nor adversity.

What was Adam's sin?

A. The sin of pride, which is the origin of dis-obedience, and from which, as Holy Scripture tells us, every sin has its beginning (Eccl. x. 14).

What were the punishments of original sin?

A. Expulsion from the terrestrial Paradise, the death of the body, all the infirmities and miseries of this life, and the loss of all the other supernatural gifts of which we have spoken. Being deprived of sanctifying grace, they stood deprived also of the right which they formerly had to eternal glory, and condemned to eternal death.

Is Adam's sin inherited by all his descendants?

A. It is an article of the Faith. Not only was Adam, by his sin, subjected to the said punishments, but also all his descendants, with the exception of the Blessed Virgin Mary.

Why is the Blessed Virgin excepted?

A. Because this pious belief always obtained in the Church; and it is now defined as an irrefragable dogma, by the Bull *Ineffabilis Deus*, of His Holi-ness Pius IX.; for which cause, should any one

now deny, or cast any doubt on the immunity
of the Blessed Virgin from original sin, he would
be a heretic.

But has the Pope, by himself, authority to define
dogma?

A. The Pope has, by himself alone, authority
to define dogma (see chap. i. Of the Sources of
Theology, § v.). Observe, however, that this
definition was preceded by the vote of all the
Bishops of the Catholic world, and was accepted,
not only with submission, but also with exultation
by all the Churches of the world, who, together
with the Church of Rome, form the Catholic or
Universal Church. Hence, no one, without being
manifestly heretical, can deny or even doubt that
the Blessed Virgin Mary was Immaculate in her
Conception.

How can it be that Adam's descendants should
be justly subjected to suffer the penalty of a sin
which they had not personally committed?

A. This is somewhat of a mystery. It is enough
for us to know that God is just, and that he cannot
punish save the guilty. It would be necessary to
know clearly the nature of, or what constitutes original sin, in order to be able to see how just it is
that we should bear the punishment of it. If you
know little of the nature of a crime which the sovereign punishes, you will, perhaps, be tempted to say
that his rigour is excessive; but you would not have
had this suspicion, had you seen and examined the

trial of the criminal. We believe by faith that God cannot exceed in rigour, and this is enough for us. Original sin is transmitted to us through carnal generation ; how this transmission comes to pass, how it is imputed to us, has not yet been defined by the Church ; but this obscurity in which we find ourselves can give us no right to doubt a truth which is of faith. Can you say that a thing is not because you do not know or understand how it is ?

Then children who die without baptism are there-fore condemned to eternal death ?

A. We cannot doubt it ; not, however, in the same way in which Adam and Eve would have suf-fered eternal death, had they not repented. In them this sin was a sin committed by the malice of their own will : not so with us their descendants. Hence, theologians almost universally believe that such children suffer no other pain than that of being deprived of the vision of God ; and St. Thomas is of opinion that they will not be sensible even of this pain. This opinion of St. Thomas is embraced by most grave and sound authors, and is therefore very probable. According to this opinion, eternal death for those children would consist in the simple deprivation of eternal life, without sorrow or suffer-ing. Observe, moreover, that there being no neces-sity why God should reveal to us how He punishes original sin in such children, we ought not to marvel that He has not revealed it to us.

SECT. IV. *Paradise, Purgatory, and Hell.*

Is it an article of the Faith that there is a Paradise?

A. It is an article of the Faith, expressed in the Creed, under the name of Eternal Life.

Where is Paradise?

A. Paradise is in Heaven : " Be glad and rejoice, for your reward is very great in Heaven" (St. Matt. v. 12); and it is a place of so great beauty, riches, and magnificence, that in this world we can form no adequate idea of it. Every shadow of evil is completely excluded from Paradise, and every kind of good is found there.

What do the saints enjoy in Paradise?

A. Their Essential Beatitude consists in seeing and loving God. In contemplating His Infinite Beauty, clearly manifested to their intellects as it is in itself, and in loving His Infinite Goodness, with a love which causes them to taste it in its own proper sweetness, consists that blessedness which, as St. Paul says,—" Eye hath not seen, nor ear heard, neither hath it entered into the heart of man to conceive" (1 Cor. ii. 9).

Why do you say *Essential* Beatitude?

A. Because this Beatitude is so great and complete, that with it alone the Saints are so blessed that they cannot desire anything else. They enjoy, moreover, the material beauty of Heaven, the society of the Saints their companions, and that of the Angels, the presence of Mary, the Queen of Heaven, and, above all, of the Sacred Humanity of Jesus Christ: but this joy being in no way necessary to perfect beatitude, it may be called *accidental*, or accessory joy. In Heaven, moreover, are given certain accidental rewards, which are called *Aureoles*, that is to say, coronets, as distinct from the *Aurea*, or Crown of Eternal Glory common to all the Blessed. St. Thomas defines these Aureoles as "a joy, or accidental reward, added to the essential reward, or joy, for some extraordinary victory." He says further, that there are three kinds of Aureoles: the first, those of Virgins, who, overcoming the flesh, live the lives of Angels in human bodies; the second, those of Martyrs, who overcome the world with all its terrors, and all human respect; the third, those of Doctors, who overcome the Devil, discovering his frauds, and driving him from men's souls. Observe that these Aureoles are called *coronets*, not because they are small in themselves, for their splendour and value are immense; but they are called *coronets*, or small, in comparison with the *Aurea*, that is to say, in comparison with the Essential Beatitude which is common to all the Blessed. In the same way, we should call the greatest treasure in the world small, compared to a high mountain of gold, or to a sea shore composed of gems. The glory of those crowns, although it will be specially in the *souls* of the Blessed, will also redound to their glorified bodies after the resurrection, as the same St. Thomas affirms.

Will the Blessed be secure of not losing Paradise for all eternity?

A. They will be perfectly secure; and it is this certainty which makes their Beatitude complete, knowing that whatever they then enjoy they will enjoy for ever.

Is it an article of the Faith that there is a Purgatory?

A. It is an article of the Faith, always acknowledged as such by all Catholics, and finally declared to be so by the most Holy Council of Trent. In Purgatory satisfaction is made for every debt of *temporal* punishment which we owe to the Divine Justice for venial sins, and also for mortal sins, already pardoned as far as regards their guilt and the *eternal* punishment which they have merited. We shall see afterwards, in its proper place, how mortal sins, which are pardoned so far as regards their guilt and the eternal punishment due to them, must still be satisfied for by some *temporal* punishment, either by good works and Indulgences in this life, or else in Purgatory.

What kind of pain do the Holy Souls suffer in Purgatory?

A. The pain of fire, which will be most fierce, for as St. Augustine says (on Psalm 37), the fire of Purgatory is sharper than any pain that can be experienced on earth; they suffer also the still greater pain of seeing themselves deprived of the Vision of God, after which souls separated from the body ardently aspire.

Is it an article of the Faith, that in Purgatory there is *material* fire?

A. It is not an article of the Faith, and some have thought that Purgatory is a place of darkness, full of sadness, but without fire; but the common opinion of Theologians, as Bellarmine proves, is contrary to this opinion, and therefore, as we have said in the 1st Chapter, 6th Sect., we must hold it as a certain and undeniable fact, that there is in Purgatory true material fire.

Do the souls in Purgatory remain there for a long time?

A. The time is proportioned to the temporal punishments for which they are debtors to the Divine Justice; hence some souls remain there for a longer, some for a shorter time. The Church desires that pious bequests for the souls of the departed should still be fulfilled, even for centuries after their death; and thus makes known to us her belief, that there are some souls in Purgatory who must there remain suffering for an immense time. Observe, that at the day of the Universal Judgment Purgatory will be at an end, and should there then be some souls who ought to remain a yet longer time, in order to satisfy for their debts, God will cause that in a shorter time they shall suffer more intense pains, and so be more quickly purged; in order that all the elect may, on that day ascend glorious and blessed into Heaven.

Are the souls in Purgatory certain of their eternal salvation?

A. They are most certain of it. Luther taught the contrary error; but it was condemned, with his other errors, by Pope Leo X.

Are the souls in Purgatory resigned to the Divine Will, in so much pain?

A. They are perfectly resigned, and although they suffer most grievous pain, they sleep the sleep of peace, being perfectly conformed to the Divine Will, loving God and His adorable dispensations with the intense affection of charity.

Where is Purgatory?

A. It is the common opinion of the Doctors of the Church, that Purgatory is in the bowels of the earth.

Can the living afford relief to the souls in Purgatory?

A. This is an article of the Faith, as declared by the most Holy Council of Trent. The means by which they can afford them relief, are works of mortification, prayers made in their behalf, and the application of such Indulgences as are applicable to them; but above all, the souls of Purgatory are succoured by the Holy Sacrifice of the Mass, as the Council of Trent declares.

Is it an article of the Faith that there is a Hell?

A. It is an article of the Faith, as declared by several General Councils. By Hell is meant a place of torment, where the devils, and sinners who die stained with mortal sin, are punished. This place of torment will never have an end, nor can the devils or the damned be ever liberated from it.

Is it also an article of the Faith, that the pains of the devils and of the damned will never come to an end?

A. It is as much an article of the Faith as the existence of Hell; and is affirmed by the same General Councils.

What are the principal pains of Hell?

A. Fire, privation of the Vision of God, and eternal despair; the damned being most certain that their pains will never end.

Will the damned all suffer equal pain?

A. No; it would be contrary to the Justice of God. As in Heaven, the Blessed have divers degrees of glory according to the diversity of their merits, so in Hell, the damned have diverse degrees of pain, according to the diversity of their demerits. Although all who are in Hell are most miserable, still the pain they suffer is more or less intense, according to the number and gravity of their sins.

Do the devils and the damned ever come out of Hell?

A. It is the opinion of Theologians, that some devils, by the permission of God, inhabit the regions of the air; founding on the authority of St. Paul who calls them: *Rectores tenebrarum harum . . . in cælestibus.* "The Rulers of the world of this darkness, the spirits of wickedness in the high places" (Ephes. vi. 12): but the permanent place assigned to them is Hell, from which they, as well as the souls of the damned, can issue, for some just cause permitted by God. Observe, however, that when they do come out of Hell, they are not freed from the pains which they suffer there, and which accompany them in every place. Further it is certain that, after the General Judgment, they will never more be able to quit Hell. It is an undeniable fact, from many facts related in history, that devils and souls of the damned do sometimes come out of Hell.

SECT. V. *The Consummation of the World.*

When will the consummation of the world arrive?

A. It is most uncertain, nor is there any argument to prove with certainty whether it will happen shortly, or after many ages. Moreover, such an enquiry appears useless, Jesus Christ having said that the Angels know nothing of that day, and that hour, in which the world shall come to an end; nay! that in regard to His Humanity not even He Himself knows it (Mark xiii. 32); knowing it only, as St. Gregory the Great says, by reason of His Divinity, and not choosing to manifest it. Hence it is not to be wondered at, if various ancient authors, famous for learning and sanctity, wishing to fix the epoch of the Consummation of the World were deceived. Wisely, therefore, did St. Thomas set himself to combat every conjecture made by men on this point; and St. Alphonsus de Liguori in the work from which we have already quoted (DISS. v.), concludes thus : "What is certain is what Jesus Christ said : De die autem illâ, et horâ nemo scit. Of that day, and of that hour no man knoweth." Moreover, Leo X., in the Lateran Council, expresses himself as follows : "Tempus quoque præfixum futurorum malorum, vel Antichristi adventum, aut certam diem Judicii prædicare, vel asserere quis nequaquam præsumat." "Let no man presume to lay down, or set forth the time appointed of the coming evils, or the advent of Antichrist, or the certain day of the Judgment."

Will Antichrist precede the end of the world ?

A. It is the teaching of all the Holy Fathers, and the sentiment of the Faithful in all ages, that Antichrist will certainly precede the end of the world. Holy Scripture also speaks clearly on this point, in several passages.

Who will Antichrist be ?

A. Antichrist will be a most wicked man, who will have commerce with the devil, will work false prodigies, will seek to make himself adored as God, will persecute Catholics more cruelly than they have ever yet been persecuted, and who will have a great number of followers. He will be the

author of great devastation and ruin ; and in his
time the public celebration of the Divine Mysteries,
particularly of the Holy Mass, will cease.

Who will come to preach against him ?

A. Enoch and Elias, who, according to the
common opinion of Catholics, are yet living. They
will preserve many Catholics from error, and will
convert many infidels, especially Jews, who before the end of the world will detest their obstinate
perfidy, and acknowledge Jesus Christ. Enoch and
Elias will crown their preaching at last by martyrdom.

Will other signs precede the end of the world ?

A. Many terrible signs described in the Holy
Gospels, such as tempests, earthquakes, famines,
pestilences, disturbance of the seasons, &c., will
precede the end of the world.

What will be the end of the world ?

A. It will end by a prodigious fire, which will
consume everything on this earth, and by which
even the Heavens being on fire shall be dissolved,
as St. Peter says (2 St. Peter. iii., 10, 12, 13).

Is it an article of the Faith that the bodies of
men will rise again at the end of the world ?

A. It is an Article of the Faith, as expressed in
the Creed by the words: "The Resurrection of
the Flesh."

Will all men rise again, without exception ?

A. We must except the Most Blessed Virgin
Mary, who rose again soon after her death ; a

truth most certain on the authority of the Holy
Fathers and Doctors, as well as by the sentiment
of the whole Catholic Church, which celebrates with
the greatest solemnity Her glorious Assumption into
Heaven. We must also except Enoch and Elias,
who will rise again three days and a half after their
martyrdom, as we read in the Apocalypse (ch.
xi., v. 11, 12). St. Thomas and Maldonatus except
also the Saints who rose again, at the time of our
Lord's death (Matt. xxvii. 52). With these except-
tions, there is no doubt that all men will rise again,
for all men must die, and afterwards present themselves with their bodies at the Universal Judgment.

.But if all men must die before they present themselves at the Judgment, why is Jesus Christ called
the Judge of the Living and the Dead?

A. St. Thomas answers, that by the living, are
meant those who will remain alive up to the last day
of the world. Nevertheless, they too will die, because
of the condemnation pronounced by God against
all the children of Adam. But, being alive a few
hours before the Universal Judgment, their death
is scarcely considered, and it is said that they will
go, as it were alive, to Judgment, because they have
remained in life up to the extremity of time, which
ends with the judgment.

Since all men will rise again, will they rise with
the same bodies which they had formerly?

A. This is an article of the Faith. Were they to
rise again with other bodies, how could it be said

7

that the flesh, or the bodies which were dead, rose again. The bodies of the damned will rise horrible and frightful, although in their natural form. The bodies of the Blessed will also rise in their natural form, but most beautiful and glorious, endowed, moreover, with the four qualities which belong to glorified bodies : Brightness, Impassibility, Agility, and Subtility.

Explain to me those qualities.

A. *Brightness* signifies a splendour, of most vivid light, with which they will shine as suns ; *Impassibility* will render them immortal and incapable of suffering the least pain or inconvenience ; *Agility* will render them most prompt in corresponding with the desires of the soul, for the bodies of the Blessed being without weight or heaviness, they will transport themselves from one place to another with the most rapid motion. By the gift of *Subtility* they will be freed from all density, as St. Alphonsus expresses it, in such sort that the soul will govern the body as if it were a spirit, not because it will become a spirit or an ethereal body, but because the body will be perfectly obedient to the soul.

What will be the stature of the rising bodies ?

A. St. Thomas says, that men will rise with the stature which they had, or would have had at the natural termination of the increase of the body. Those, however, who were, or might have been, of defective stature, from being immoderately tall or short, will by the Divine Omnipotence have these defects supplied, that they may rise again of an ordinary stature.

In what place will the Universal Judgment be held?

A. The general opinion of the Doctors teaches that the Universal Judgment will take place in the Valley of Jehoshaphat. There the Elect will be placed on the Right, and the reprobate on the Left.

What will be the Sign of the Son of Man which will appear, according to the prediction in the Gospel of St. Matthew, ch. xxiv., v. 30?

A. According to the common opinion of the Holy Fathers and Doctors, this Sign will be the resplendent Cross of our Lord Jesus Christ, that is to say, either the very same Cross on which He died, or, as is more probable, an image of His Cross.

Will Jesus Christ descend in human form, to judge men?

A. It is certain and undoubted that, as in human form He ascended into Heaven, so He will descend thence in human form, and that with great power and majesty, as is revealed in the Holy Gospels.

How will the Judgment proceed?

A. Jesus Christ will cause all the good works of the just, and all the evil deeds of the damned to be made manifest; so that each one will know clearly his own merits or demerits, and in like manner will see the merits or demerits of others. In that day the admirable conduct of the Divine Justice in regard to all men will be seen.

How will the sentence be given?

A. After all things shall have been thus made known, Jesus Christ will invite all the Elect to Paradise, and will condemn all the reprobate to Hell. Then shall the Elect, as in a most glorious triumph, ascend into Heaven, there to rest for ever; whilst the earth opening under the feet of the reprobate, they shall be engulfed by Hell, from whence neither the damned nor the devils shall ever any more issue forth.

Will there then be the consummation of the world?

A. Such will be the end of this World, that is to say, the series of vicissitudes amidst which the children of Adam live. Oh! that whilst we are in time, we might know the vanity of all transitory, and the importance of all eternal things, so that, in that great day, we might receive a favourable sentence from Christ the Judge.

Will our earth, the sun and stars, cease to exist?

A. The earth cannot cease to exist since it contains in its bosom Hell, which will never end; neither will the sun and stars cease to exist, but they will shine with a more beautiful and brilliant light. St. John, in the Apocalypse, saw a new heaven and a new earth (Apoc. xxi., 1). All will therefore be renewed in a better form by the Omnipotence of God.

But what will be the use of the surface of the earth, and of the sun and stars, when all the elect will be in Paradise, and all the reprobate in Hell?

A. Holy Scripture tells us nothing on this head ; nor can we imagine anything probable about it. Therefore let us turn all our curiosity to the search after those means, whereby we may secure to ourselves the possession of Heaven. There we shall see all things; and in all things, and for all things we shall give to God eternal praise.

CHAPTER IV.

THE INCARNATION OF THE SON OF GOD.

SECT. I. *Notion of the Mystery.*

How do you define the mystery of the Incarnation?

A. It is a primary mystery of the Christian religion, whereby the Eternal Word assumed inseparably, in the unity of His Person, a true and entire human nature, in order to appease Almighty God by His sufferings, and to reconcile Him with the human race.

Why do you call it a primary mystery?

A. Because it is the foundation of the Christian religion, and the basis of all our hopes.

Why do you say that the Eternal Word did this?

. A. To express that a Divine Person became incarnate, and that therefore Christ is not a mere man, but True Man and True God; and further, to denote that the Second Person of the Blessed Trinity alone became incarnate, and not the Father, nor the Holy Ghost.

Then, the Incarnation of the Son of God is not the work of all the Persons of the Blessed Trinity? The Father and the Holy Ghost did not concur to it?

A. The Incarnation of the Son of God is the work of the Divine Omnipotence; and so is the work of the Blessed Trinity. Therefore the Father and the Holy Ghost did concur to it; but the union with a human nature was made only by the Second Person, the Son alone took and assumed human flesh. To make use of a material comparison, suppose that Peter is dressing himself, whilst James and John are assisting him. Peter alone puts on the dress, but James and John co-operate and concur in the dressing of Peter.

Why do you employ the word *inseparably?*

A. Because the Word having assumed human nature, united it to Himself, so as never more to separate Himself from it: therefore, when Christ died upon the cross, the Soul of Christ was separated from His Body, but the Eternal Word was not separated either from the Body which remained in the sepulchre, nor from the Soul which descended into hell; and throughout all eternity Jesus Christ will ever be True Man and True God.

Why do you say that He assumed *human nature,* and not that He assumed *man?* Could you not say that He united man to Himself?

A. You must understand that God did not create a soul and a body, and form a man of them, and then unite Himself with that man, in the Incarnation; but He created a soul and formed a body, and assumed, or united both to His Divine Person; therefore, the Eternal Word did not take a human *person,* but a human *nature.* And anyone who should say that in Christ there are two persons, a human and a Divine, would be a heretic: in Christ there are two natures, the Divine Nature and the Human Nature, but not two persons. Christ is one only Person, that is, the Second Person of the Blessed Trinity.

Why would it be heresy to say that in Christ there are two persons, a human and a Divine?

A. Because the Church has condemned this error in Nestorius. Nestorius maintained that Christ consisted of two persons, a human and a Divine, united together by the bond of charity; and so he would not have the Blessed Virgin called the Mother of God, because, according to his error, she was mother only of the human person of Christ.

Mary, then, is the true Mother of God?

A. This is an article of the Faith, because in the Womb of Mary there became incarnate, and of her there was born, a Divine Person, Jesus Christ.

Admitting that in Jesus Christ there is one Person alone, might we not also say that in Him there is one nature alone?

A. This would be the heresy condemned in Eutyches. The Church has defined, as an article of the Faith, that in Christ there are two Natures, a Human and a Divine, and only one Divine Person, as we have already said; and this is what we must firmly believe and profess.

What consequences follow from these truths?

A. That in Christ we must admit, what is called by theologians a *Communicatio idiomatum*, by which the properties and attributes which belong to the Human Nature, as well as those which belong to the Divine Nature, are attributed to Jesus Christ. And so we say that Jesus Christ was *born*, and we say that He is *eternal:* He was born, because His Humanity had Its beginning in the womb of the Virgin Mary; He is eternal because His Divinity has existed from all eternity. We say that He is *limited*, and we say that He is *Immense*: He is limited because His Humanity is limited; He is Immense because His Divinity is Immense; and so of the other properties of the two natures.

Can we say, then, that the Humanity of Christ is Immense, and that His Divinity is limited?

A. No. Speaking absolutely of Christ, who is one only Divine Person, and has two distinct natures, we may speak of Him inasmuch as He is God, and inasmuch as He is Man; but when we speak of His Divinity or of His Humanity, separately, then we may not admit this reciprocal communication; and so we must say that the Humanity of Christ is limited, and that His Divinity is Immense; that His Humanity had Its beginning in time, and that His Divinity is eternal, &c.

What other consequences follow from these truths?

A. That Christ must be called the Son of God by nature, and not the Son of God by adoption, not even inasmuch as He is Man; and so the Church has defined, in opposition to certain heretics, that Christ is to be adored with the supreme worship of *Latria*, and not with the worship of

Dulia, or *Hyperdulia,* with which we adore the Saints, and the Blessed Virgin, respectively ; that the actions of Christ had an infinite merit ; that the Virgin Mary is true Mother of God; and other con-sequences, which you will find in theological writers.

If the Blessed Virgin Mary is to be called the Mother of God, because in Her womb the Son of God became incarnate, we must call the Holy Ghost the Father of God, because it was by His operation that the Son of God became incarnate in the womb of the Virgin Mary.

A. That one be called father, it is necessary that he contribute of his substance to his son ; now the Holy Ghost did not contribute the substance, for the formation of the Body of the Incarnate Word. The Blessed Virgin alone ministered this substance, and from Her most pure blood, by virtue of the Holy Ghost, was formed the Body of Jesus Christ.

Why do you say further that Christ took a true and *entire* human nature ?

A. In order to avoid the error of those heretics who taught, that Christ took a body which was ethereal and in appearance only, and so did not take true human flesh. Also to indicate that He took a true, rational human soul, in opposition to the error of those other heretics, who imagined that Christ had taken only a body ; or, admitting that he had taken a soul, imagined that it was not a human, that is a rational soul,—but that in Christ the Eternal Word took the place of a soul.

Finally, for what reason do you say,—in order to appease God by His sufferings, and to reconcile Him with the human race?

A. These words shew the end of the Incarnation, which was to free men from sin, and from the punishment, which sin merits; they shew also the means which Christ adopted to attain this end, to wit, His Passion and Death, by which the Divine Justice was appeased in regard to us.

Did Christ suffer really, that is to say, did He really feel those interior and exterior pains, which He appeared to suffer?

A. It is as much an article of the Faith that Christ really suffered, as that He took true human flesh. The Eternal Word took a Human Body, subject to hunger and weariness, to wounds and pain, passible and mortal; and He truly suffered all that the Holy Evangelists relate of His Sufferings. He took, moreover, a Human Soul, which was capable of sadness, heaviness, and affliction, like the souls of other men; with this difference, that we suffer sadness, heaviness, and afflictions which very often we can neither alleviate nor remove, by our own will; whereas the Soul of Christ ruled as Lord over these passions, and suffered them only in that degree which He willed.

Is it of faith that Christ has merited for us the pardon of our sins, the graces necessary for salvation, and that He has restored to us the right to eternal life, which we had lost?

A. These are truths of the Faith. Jesus Christ, by His humiliations and sufferings, has not only merited for Himself, as St. Paul says (Phil. ii.), the Glory of His Body and the Exaltation of His Name, but He has also merited for us every supernatural grace ; and He has merited them, not only for those who have lived since the time of His Incarnation, but also for those who lived before that time ; so that all the supernatural graces bestowed upon men, even before His Incarnation, were merited for them by Jesus Christ ; that is to say, they obtained them in regard of the merits of Jesus Christ, Who was to come, in order to make satisfaction for the sins of the whole world, and to obtain for men every good availing to eternal life.

If He has merited eternal life for all men, do you mean to say that all men will be saved ?

A. He has merited eternal life for all men, but He requires the co-operation of men, in order to their obtaining the same. He has not merited for men so that they should be compelled to save themselves, but He has so merited for them, that by the help of His grace, they, willing it, may be able to save themselves. Hence, notwithstanding His superabundant merits, which are capable of saving innumerable men, more than ever existed, now exist, or shall hereafter exist, he who chooses to damn himself is damned, as we see is the case with the greater part of men, who, abusing their own liberty, are lost.

Could not God have saved men in some other way, without becoming man?

A. He could have saved us, of His Absolute Power, in other ways, but He chose this way, in order to receive an adequate satisfaction for the injury, which sin had done Him. Observe that God, of His Absolute Power, could have pardoned sin, without exacting any satisfaction, or by accepting the satisfaction which might have been offered Him by some holy creature, as, for instance, by an Angel; but this satisfaction would not have been proportionate to the injury received.

For what reason, then, did God choose this mode, rather than any other?

A. We must not seek to know the reason of God's operations; nevertheless, we may say that He chose this mode, because it was the most fitting; His Divine Justice being in this way most fully satisfied, and His other Attributes, such as His Clemency, His Wisdom, His Omnipotence, &c., being made manifest in an incomparable degree. Moreover, this was the most efficacious mode to gain our love. For, that a God should become man, and subject Himself to sufferings and to death, in order to save men, is such an excess of love as to oblige even the hardest hearts to love this God.

Was God obliged to provide a remedy of some kind, for the ruin into which sin had plunged us?

A. He might justly have abandoned us in our sin, and to the consequences of our sin; it was the work of His Infinite Mercy, to provide a remedy for our evils.

Was the Incarnation of the Son of God foretold, before it was effected ?

A. It was foretold immediately after Adam's fall, and the Prophets all spoke of it. Hence Jesus Christ was expected by the Jews ; and even the Gentiles, as we gather from profane history, were in expectation of a Saviour.

For what reason would the Jewish people not acknowledge Him when He came ?

• A. Because of their pride, and the obstinacy of their prejudices. The Jews were absolutely without excuse, for they had the Prophecies which spoke clearly of Him ; and those Prophecies they saw verified in Jesus Christ.

SECT. II. *The Body and Soul of Christ.*

Can we say that the Body of Jesus Christ consists of human flesh ; and that therefore He became a son of Adam ?

A. We have already declared it to be a Catholic truth, that Christ took true and real human flesh, like that of other men, with this difference—that He did not take It by the operation of man, but by the operation of the Holy Ghost ; therefore, having taken true and real human flesh, He became a son of Adam.

Was not St. Joseph, the Husband of Mary, the Father of Jesus ?

A. St. Joseph was the Husband of Mary; but he remained ever a virgin, and left the Blessed Mary ever a virgin. It would be heresy to say that St. Joseph was the true father of Jesus Christ; he was only the reputed father, that is, believed to be such by persons who, knowing that he had espoused and lived with Mary, and seeing that she had a son, thought that she had had him by Joseph. On the contrary, however, St. Joseph always lived with Mary, as if he had been Her brother, and nothing more.

How could the Blessed Mary have had a son, whilst she remained a Virgin?

A. This is a miracle of the Omnipotence of God; and so great a miracle that none has ever taken place like it. The Holy Ghost, as we have already mentioned, formed the Body of Jesus Christ, of the most pure blood of Mary; in due time Mary brought Him forth in the stable of Bethlehem, remaining even then a Virgin as before; and so she brought Him forth without pain or sorrow, and without any injury or violation of her virginal integrity. Observe that it is an Article of the Faith, that Mary was a Virgin before childbirth, in childbirth, and after childbirth, as defined by the General Council of Chalcedon.

In the Holy Gospel mention is made of the *Brethren* of Jesus Christ; does it mean that the Blessed Mary had other children?

A. The Blessed Mary had no other children.

The Jews called other relations by the name of brethren; these, therefore, were relations of Jesus Christ, but not His true brothers.

How did the death of Jesus Christ occur?

A. His Soul was separated from His Body, as happens when men die; His Divinity, that is, the Eternal Word, however, remaining united, as we have already said, both to His Body and to His Soul.

During the time that the Body of Christ remained in the Sepulchre, did It begin to corrupt, as do other dead bodies?

A. The Body of Jesus Christ suffered no corruption in the sepulchre, as the Prophet David had foretold. (Ps. xv.)

For how long did the Body of Christ remain in the sepulchre?

A. Part of Friday, the whole of Saturday, and part of Sunday. On the morning of Sunday His Soul was re-united to His Body, Which rose Glorious, Immortal, and Impassible. Thus risen, He appeared several times to His disciples, and forty days after His Resurrection He ascended into Heaven.

When the Eternal Word became man, did He take a Soul, of the same nature as our Soul?

A. It is an article of the Faith, as we have already shewn, that the Eternal Word took a Human Soul, and therefore of the same nature as ours.

Are we to acknowledge a *Human* Will in Christ, besides the Divine Will?

A. It is an Article of the Faith that we are to acknowledge a Human Will in Christ, which, although free like ours, was nevertheless always conformed to the Divine Will, the Soul of Christ never having willed other than was willed by the Eternal Word. The Church defined this Article of the Faith, in opposition to an ancient sect of heretics—the Monothelites.

Must we acknowledge human operations in Christ, besides the Divine operations?

A. Christ being not only True God but also True Man, we must certainly acknowledge human operations in Him. In fact, when we read in the Holy Gospels that Christ suffered hunger and weariness, that He wept, that He was sorrowful, &c., we at once understand that these are human operations. Moreover, the Human Operations of Christ have an Infinite Merit, because, by virtue of the Hypostatic Union, they were the actions of a Divine Person.

Was the Soul of Christ endowed with knowledge?

A. The Soul of Christ, from the first moment of Its creation, had a full and most perfect knowledge of all things ; and although, as Christ grew in age, He appeared, as the Gospel observes, to grow in wisdom, it was not really so, since He had always possessed the fulness of wisdom. Moreover, the Soul of Christ enjoyed the Intuitive Vision of God, even as the Saints enjoy it in Paradise, beholding clearly the Person of the Eternal Word, with Which It was hypostatically united, and, necessarily, along with the Person of the Eternal Word, It beheld the

8

Person of the Father, and the Person of the Holy Ghost.

If the Soul of Christ beheld God clearly, It must have been Blessed, and incapable of suffering. How then can the Catholic dogma, that Christ really suffered in His Passion and Death, consist with this Vision of God, attributed to Christ?

A. It is true that the Beatific Vision of God renders the soul incapable of suffering ; but, by a great miracle of the Divine Omnipotence, the joy which the Vision of God occasioned in the superior, that is, in the intellectual part of His Soul, was held in check and restrained, so to speak, in order that it might not be communicated to the inferior, that is, to the sensitive part of His Soul, and that so It might be capable of suffering. Hence He truly suffered both interior and exterior pains, as the Gospel teaches us.

Can you explain this to me better, by some example?

A. Observe what happens on very high mountains. Sometimes the clouds thicken and tempests gather half way up the mountain, whilst the sun shines on the summit. Thus he who is on the summit of the mountain enjoys a serene sky, whilst he who is on its sides is enveloped in clouds and tossed by the tempest. According to our mode of understanding, the same thing took place in the Soul of Christ ; the superior, that is the intellectual part, enjoyed the clear Vision of God, the inferior, that is the sensitive part, suffered every kind of sorrow and pain.

The Soul of Christ beheld and knew God, more clearly than any other creature whatsoever can know Him ; was It able therefore to comprehend, that is, to know God, as He comprehends and knows Himself?

A. We have already shown (Ch. ii., Sect. 4), that, God being Incomprehensible, no creature can comprehend Him ; and as, although the Soul of Christ had a more clear knowledge of Him than any other creature, yet It did not comprehend, that is, did not know God with that fulness of knowledge, with which God knows Himself.

Was the Soul of Christ endowed with liberty?

A. Undoubtedly; otherwise Its operations would not have been human actions ; and It would have been diverse in nature from the nature of our souls.

Could He sin?

A. Being hypostatically united with the Eternal Word, He could not sin ; on the contrary, He had a grace, called the Grace of Union, or Substantial Grace, whereby He was Holy *substantially.*

Had He sanctifying grace?

A. He had it in its highest degree, which without comparison exceeded the grace of all the angels, of all the saints, and of the Blessed Virgin herself.

Were all the virtues in Christ?

A. Undoubtedly, except those which presuppose sin, or other imperfection. He could not therefore possess the virtue of Penance, for there was in Him nothing of which He could repent; nor the virtues of Faith and Hope, because these virtues cannot be present in a soul which enjoys the intuitive Vision of God.

When Christ died on the Cross, and His Soul was separated from His Body, did It descend into hell?

A. This is an article of the Faith, and expressed in the Creed. Observe, however, that here, under the name of Hell, is not meant the hell destined for the devils and the damned, but the subterranean regions, commonly called Limbus, where the Holy Souls of all the Just, who had died before the coming of Christ, reposed, and there waited till the Gates of Paradise should be opened to them, by the completion of the work of redemption.

Then the Just, who died before the period of the death of Christ, did not enjoy the Vision of God in Heaven?

A. They did not; but they reposed, in the most perfect peace and tranquillity, in Limbus. Thither the Soul of Christ descended, and freed them from this prison, in order to conduct them to Heaven.

SECT. III. *The various Titles which belong to Christ; the Worship due to Him, and that which belongs to His Saints.*

What titles belong to Christ?

A. 1. He is the Son of God *by nature;* not even considering Him as Man, can He be called the

Son of God *by adoption.* 2. He is a King, not only according to His Divinity, but according to His Humanity. 3. He is the Head of men and of angels. 4. He is a Lawgiver. 5. He is a Judge. 6. He is a Priest, and a Priest for ever. 7. He is the Mediator or Reconciler between God and men, having fully, nay, superabundantly made satisfaction to the Divine Justice for them.

Does Christ pray for us to His Father?

A. St. Augustine says that Christ, as Man, prays for us, and that as God, He, along with the Divine Father, hears our prayer ; *Christus homo pro nobis est orator; ut Deus est cum Patre exauditor.* Christ as man prays for us ; and, as God, He, with the Father, hears our prayers.

What worship is due to Christ ?

A. Observe that there are three kinds of worship. The first is that of *Latria*, which is the supreme and absolute adoration wherewith we adore God, by reason of His Uncreated and Infinite Excellence. The second is the worship of *Dulia*, which is the adoration with which we venerate certain creatures, for their supernatural, but not supremely, or singularly excellent, dignity. The third is the worship of *Hyperdulia*, which is the adoration with which we honour a creature for her supernatural, and singularly excellent dignity. Observe this, it is of faith that Christ, God and Man, is to be adored with the adoration of *Latria;* and that, with the same adoration of *Latria* His Humanity is also to be adored, not by reason of itself, but by reason of the Uncreated and Infinite Excellence of the Eternal Word, with which it is personally and substantially united.

To whom is the worship of *Dulia* due ? ·

A. It is due to the angels and saints, who possess a supernatural dignity, but not in a *singular* degree of excellence.

To whom is the worship of *Hyperdulia* due ?

A. This pertains to the Blessed Virgin Mary alone, who enjoys a supernatural dignity in a singular degree of excellence, She being, as we have already said, the true Mother of God.

Is it meet that we venerate the saints, the angels, and the Blessed Virgin ?

A. It is most meet, as it is always most meet to honour the friends, the ministers, and much more, the Mother of the Sovereign. Earthly sovereigns, when they see their friends, ministers, or mothers honoured, reckon this honour as if paid to themselves. In like manner God is honoured by the honour rendered to the saints, to the angels, and to the Blessed Virgin Mary.

Is it useful to have recourse to the Intercession of the Saints, the Angels, and the Blessed Virgin Mary ?

A. It is most useful ; for they hear our prayers, they are most zealous for our welfare, and they obtain for us the graces which we need. Above all, it is most useful to have recourse to the intercession of Mary, for Her prayers are so powerful with Her Divine Son, that one prayer of Hers is of more value

than the prayers of all the Angels and Saints in
Paradise combined. The Church has always promoted, with singular earnestness, devotion to the
Blessed Virgin, and this devotion consists in vene-
rating Her, and in praying to Her to intercede for us.
The Saints who have been most eminent for knowledge and piety, were ever distinguished by a most
special devotion to Mary. The authors who enjoy
the reputation of the soundest and most stainless
doctrine, have ever written great things of devotion to Mary; Her worship is disapproved only by
heretics; and those who have little devotion to Her
are those only who are not good Christians. I ask
pardon of Mary, I ask pardon of Her devout clients
when I say merely, that devotion to Her is most
useful; for more than this might be said without
fear of error.

Do those who say that Mary bestows graces
express themselves correctly?

A. They express themselves well, because the
Church asks Mary to bestow graces, *Solve vincla
reis, profer lumen cœcis*, &c. Break the bonds of
the captive, give light to the darkened, &c. Understand, however, that Mary *impetrates* these graces
for us, it being certain that the *Author* of all grace,
as the Author of all good, is God alone.

What points are expressly defined as of Faith, in
regard to the worship of the Saints?

A. The sacred Council of Trent, in the 25 Sess.,
declares it to be of Faith that the Saints pray for us

before God ; and that it is a good and a useful thing suppliantly to invoke them.   Hence he who should deny this truth would be a heretic.

Are the Images of the Saints to be venerated ?

A. It is of the Faith, as defined in the Second Council of Nice, and in the Council of Trent, that Holy Images are to be venerated, referring however the worship which is rendered to them, either to Christ, or to the Blessed Virgin, or to the Saints whom they represent.

Are the Relics of the Saints to be venerated ?

A. The sacred Council of Trent expressly defines that veneration and honour are due to the Relics of the Saints.   Observe moreover, that among all Relics, the Wood of the True Cross of Christ merits a special veneration, as the most precious Relic which remains to us of our Saviour.

CHAPTER V.

THE GRACE OF GOD.

SECT. I. *The notions of the different kinds of Grace, and particularly, of Actual Grace.*

WHAT do you mean by the Grace of Christ?

A. A supernatural gift of God which, in regard of the merits of Jesus Christ, is conferred upon man gratuitously, in order that he may attain to his supernatural end, which is eternal salvation. From this definition you will perceive, that under the name of the Grace of Christ we do not intend to speak of natural graces, such, for example, as health, or a good understanding; nor yet of the grace bestowed upon the first man in the estate of innocence, and upon the Angels; but of the *medicinal* grace of the Saviour, which is bestowed upon man, since his fall by original sin, in regard of the merits of the same Saviour.

How is this grace divided?

A. It is divided into external grace, internal grace, and grace *gratis data*. External graces are the example of Christ, the preaching of the Holy Gospel, &c. Internal graces are good inspirations, the gifts of the Holy Ghost, &c. Graces *gratis datæ* are those which are given to a man, not so much for his own personal advantage, as for the benefit of others; such as the gifts of prophecy, discerning of spirits, miracles, &c. But the grace of which we would more particularly speak at present, is that which is called in the schools *gratia interna gratum faciens (internal grace making gracious)*, which is a supernatural gift particularly directed to the spiritual well-being of him on whom it is bestowed. This is divided into *Actual* grace ; and *Sanctifying*, or *Habitual* grace.

What is Actual Grace ?

A. By Actual Grace we mean those aids called *transient* in the schools, or, as we should say, passing, transitory, momentary aids, with which God, from time to time, aids our weakness, so that we may do good and avoid evil, in order to the salvation of our souls.

What is *Sanctifying* or *Habitual* grace ?

A. Sanctifying grace is a supernatural gift of God, which is permanent and inherent in our souls, by way of a habit, and by means of which a man becomes just and the friend of God, and so a son of God by adoption, an adopted brother of Jesus Christ, and an heir of Paradise.

Could you, by some comparison, explain to me more clearly the difference, which exists between Actual grace and Sanctifying grace ?

A. Picture to yourself a little child who has fallen down in the mire. This child has not the power to get up again of himself, and he has need of dry, clean clothes, because his clothes are all wet and soiled with mud. His mother hastens to his assistance, and first gives him her hand to help him up, and then dresses him again, as there is need. Here you have a twofold aid from the mother corresponding to the twofold necessity of the child; but the first is a passing, transitory, momentary aid, since when the mother helps him up, she does nothing which remains on him, to use a material expression; the second, however, is a permanent aid, since the fresh clothes, with which she covers him, remain on the child. In the help which the mother gives her child to get up again, you have a similitude of Actual grace; in the clothes which she puts upon him, you have a similitude of Habitual grace. The first is transitory; the second is permanent, remaining with a man.

Is Actual Grace necessary to man?

A. It is a dogma of the Faith, that, without the supernatural grace of God, man can do no good work contributing to Eternal Life. We must therefore say, that actual grace is most necessary, since we cannot do the very least good action contributing to the salvation of our souls, unless this grace moves us, that is, unless it excites us in the beginning, and accompanies us in the course of our actions, and even to the end. It is necessary, not only for sinners, but also for the just, that is, for those who possess sanctifying grace. St. Augustine says that however sound the eye may be, it cannot see without light, and however just a man may be, he cannot do good without grace moving him, and accompanying him in his good and saving works.

Can we not overcome temptations without grace ?

A. Without supernatural grace we cannot overcome any temptation, from a supernatural motive, either from the love of God, or from the fear of God ; for he who overcomes temptation from either of these motives, does a good in itself saving and meritorious of eternal life.　Certain temptations, however, and particularly slight temptations, may be overcome from other motives, and in such case do not require grace.　For example, I may vanquish the temptation to steal, from fear of the punishment which the civil law inflicts ; in like manner I may vanquish the temptation to tell lies, from fear of the shame which would come upon me were my falsehood made known ; such temptations would be overcome from natural motives, and would in no way be meritorious of Eternal Life ; in this way infidels and the most hardened sinners overcome many temptations.　In general, however, we affirm that temptations are not overcome without grace, since there is an infinite number of even grave temptations, to which we might consent without fear of temporal evils ; and without this fear we might always consent, at least by complacency and in desire.

Cannot we observe all the precepts of the Natural Law without grace ?

˙ A. We cannot observe all, particularly those against which the temptations are strongest and most frequent ; hence it follows that without grace we cannot avoid all sins.

Is it necessary that the just should have a special grace, in order to enable them, in this life, to avoid all and every venial sin ?

A. It is a truth defined by the Holy Council of Trent, that not even the just can, during the whole course of their life, avoid all, even venial sins, without a special privilege from God ; and it is not certain that this privilege was ever granted to any one, except to the Blessed Virgin Mary, who was never stained with the least shadow of sin. This refers to venial sins which we commit without full advertence ; for every one who wills, can avoid all sins to which he fully adverts.

Is the grace of persevering till death in the friendship of God—that is to say, is the grace of Final Perseverance a *special* gift of God ?

A. Undoubtedly it is a special gift, for the Holy Council of Trent calls it the *great gift*.

How is Actual Grace divided ?

A. It is divided into *Efficacious* grace and *Sufficient* grace.

What is Efficacious grace ?

A. That which obtains its effect. For example, God gives me grace, in order that I may be sincerely converted to Him ; 'I do not resist this grace—on the contrary, I co-operate with it with my free will, and therefore am really converted. Here is efficacious grace—that is, grace which obtains its effect.

What is Sufficient grace ?

A. That which gives to a man sufficient strength

to do good and avoid evil, but which, being resisted by man's evil will, does not obtain its effect.

Can you explain the efficacy and sufficiency of grace in any other way?

A. Theologians have framed various systems, and have explained, some in one way, some in another, the efficacy and sufficiency of grace; but, in this most difficult matter, it will suffice for us to know what is certain and beyond possibility of doubt. It is certain, that there are *efficacious* graces—that is to say, graces which obtain their effect. It is certain, that there are graces which are only *sufficient*, and which, being resisted, do not obtain their effect. This is a truth of the Faith, defined against Jansenius. This sufficient grace must be capable of obtaining—that is, sufficient to obtain the effect for which it is given. If it did not suffice to its end it would be insufficient, and sufficient grace which is not enough—that is to say, which is not sufficient, is a contradiction. It is certain, that God sincerely wills the salvation of all men; it is certain, that without His interior and actual grace no adults can be saved; it is certain, that God will not allow them to want the true aids of grace, as means absolutely necessary for the attainment of their end—that is, of their salvation; and so we all have grace sufficient to save us, and, if we co-operate with this grace, our salvation is secure. "To every one is given light and grace, that, doing what is in him, he may save himself by giving only his consent." This is the doctrine, and these are the words of St. Catherine of Genoa, whose authority, as all know, is certainly as good as that of a theologian. Precisely, and in the full rigour of the expression, this is the belief of the whole Christian people. I confess, however, that I prefer the beautiful words of the Council of Trent before all the systems :—"God does not command what is impossible ; but commanding He warns thee to do what thou art able, and to ask for what thou art not able to do. In the meanwhile He helps thee in order that thou mayest be able. His commandments are not grievous, His yoke is sweet, His burden is light. . . . Those whom He has once justified He does not abandon, unless they first abandon Him." This is the consoling doctrine of the Holy Spirit, and all the more consoling because it is infallible.

Is *Necessitating* grace given—that is to say, grace which compels man of necessity to operate ?

A. This would be—not grace, but violence. It is an article of the Faith that grace does not take away, and does not hinder the use of man's liberty ; therefore all that is done with grace is entirely free. St. Paul says, " I can do all things in Him Who strengtheneth me "—he does not say, "in Him Who forces me." It is as much of Faith that grace has part in our good works, as it is of Faith that our free will has part in them.

Does God ever impart any grace to hardened and obstinate sinners ?

A. Even the most hardened and obstinate sinners

are never without some graces—at least remote graces, to enable them to pray and obtain mercy. If they availed themselves of these graces the grace of conversion would not be wanting to them. It is not in accordance with the common sentiment of the faithful, that God should ever wholly abandon anyone in this life, and therefore we should never despair of the salvation of anyone, as long as he lives. Moreover, this accords with the teaching of St. Paul, who, speaking to hardened and impenitent sinners, instructs them that the Benignity of God invites them to penance (Romans, ch. ii.)

What do you say with regard to infidels who have no knowledge of the true Faith, because it has never been proclaimed to them?

A. Even these have some graces, by means of which they could observe the natural law; and if they availed themselves of these graces, doing what was possible to their natural powers, aided by these graces, God would certainly, either by ordinary or extraordinary means, bring them to the knowledge of the true Faith, in order that they might be saved, as St. Thomas teaches.*

Are actual graces given to man's merits?

A. This would be a heresy clearly condemned by Holy Scripture, and by the decisions of the Church.

---

* He says further, that it arises from our negligence that grace is wanting to us :—" The primary cause of lack of grace is from ourselves. It is from his own negligence that a man has not grace."

Graces are gratuitous gifts, which God grants to whom He wills, and when He wills. (Council of Trent.)

You mean to say, then, that the good have no foundation for hoping that God exercises towards them a special providence of graces?

A. This would be another error, because, although graces cannot be merited, God nevertheless, in Holy Scripture, promises a special assistance to the good —"The eyes of the Lord are upon the just, and his ears unto their prayers" (Psalm xxxiii.). Therefore, although God is not obliged to confer graces either upon the just or upon sinners, nevertheless He who loves them that love Him (Prov. viii.) ordinarily abounds in greater graces to those who show themselves faithful to Him. I say ordinarily, because sometimes, in order more wonderfully to manifest His mercy, He confers great grace even upon great sinners. Such graces He bestowed upon David, the Magdalen, the Good Thief, &c.

SECT. II. *Sanctifying Grace.*

What is it that justifies a man?

A. Sanctifying grace, the definition of which we have already given in the answer to the fourth question of the previous section.

When is sanctifying grace acquired?

A. It is acquired in Holy Baptism.

Once acquired can it be lost?

A. It is lost by every mortal sin, because by every mortal sin we lose charity.

Once lost can it be re-acquired ?

A. It can be regained by means of the Sacrament of Penance, which was expressly instituted for the remission of sins committed after Baptism ; and even by means of charity, which includes the intention, or desire of this Sacrament, as we shall explain in the following chapter.

This sanctifying grace is perhaps' the Justice of Jesus Christ, imputed to us ?

A. To say that sanctifying grace is the identical Justic of Jeesus Christ, imputed to us, is a heresy condemned by the Council of Trent. This grace consists in a supernatural gift, not imputed, but really conferred on, and made intrinsic to our souls, and by which we are truly justified, and truly cleansed from sin.

Could we not say that sanctifying grace serves as a garment to the soul, covering it, and concealing the deformity of sin ?

A. To say so would be a heresy condemned by the same Council. Sanctifying grace is not extrinsic to the soul, as a garment is extrinsic to the body which it covers ; and by the infusion of this grace sins are not concealed or covered, but absolutely taken away and cancelled, so that their stains no longer exist. 'In the same way as, when a filthy garment is washed, the stains which were in it are not covered over, but taken away, so that they no

longer exist, God, when He justifies a man by infusion of His grace, takes away sin from his soul.

Would not Faith alone be sufficient for the justification of the soul ?

A. This would be an heretical doctrine, in like
manner condemned by the Holy Council of Trent.
Faith is only the root and foundation of justification, as the Council defines; otherwise all the
faithful would be in a state of grace, and mortal
sin would not be found, save in infidels. For the
justification of a man, good works are requisite as
well as Faith. Faith without works is dead, as St.
James says. (Ch. ii., v. 20.)

Some have thought that those only were justified,
and so that those only had sanctifying grace who
firmly believed that they had that grace, in the
same way as we must firmly believe the dogmas of
the Faith. What do you say as to this doctrine ?

A. This is also an heretical doctrine, condemned
by the Council of Trent. On the contrary, observe
that no one can firmly believe that he has this
grace, without a special revelation from God.

No one then can be certain of having sanctifying
grace ?

A. The Christian who is not conscious to himself
of mortal sin, either because he knows not that he
has ever committed it, or because, after having
fallen into sin, he has rightly confessed and detested
it, may be certain of having sanctifying grace.
This certainty, however, cannot be firm and certain,

9—2

as is the infallible certainty with which we believe
the verities of the Faith; and the reason of this is,
that God has revealed the verities of the Faith, and,
therefore, as to them there can be no deception;
but to no one has it been revealed that he has never
committed a mortal sin, or that, having committed
it, he has sufficiently confessed and detested it, so
as to obtain pardon. So that, in regard to the certainty of being in a state of grace, it is possible for
a man to deceive himself.

For what reason does God leave us in this state
of uncertainty?

A. In order that fear may be a continual spur,
stimulating us to secure more and more the possession of His grace, by the exercise of the Christian virtues, and so to increase our merits for life
eternal. We may, however, be certain of having
sanctifying grace, not indeed with infallible and
divine certainty, but with moral and human certainty. Moreover, we must guard against excessive
fear in this particular, for it would diminish our
confidence in God and our love of Him.

What is the strongest argument we can have of
our being in a state of grace?

A. Listen to St. Francis of Sales, quoted by St.
Alphonsus di Liguori, both of whom were great
theologians:—" The greatest security which we can
have in this world of being in the grace of God does
not consist in the feeling of love we may have for
Him, but in the entire and irrevocable abandon-

ment of all our affections into His Hands, and in a firm resolution never to consent to any sin, whether great or small." Let us, then, resign ourselves wholly into God's Hands; let us resolve to suffer, no matter what, rather than knowingly to offend Him in the very smallest matter, and we shall have the strongest argument which upon this earth we can have, of possessing the great treasure of sanctifying grace.

Can there be augmentation of sanctifying grace in the soul of a just man?

A. This is a truth of the Faith, defined by the Holy Council of Trent, and this augmentation is acquired by means of good works.

You mean to say, then, that sanctifying grace can be merited?

A. The grace of justification cannot be merited, it being the free gift of God; and this is of Faith. No one who is in sin can merit that God should pardon him, and enrich him with sanctifying grace; but, on the other hand, the just—that is, those who already possess sanctifying grace—can, by their good works (as we shall explain in the following section), really merit an increase of this grace.

Is sanctifying grace necessary to good works?

A. It is necessary, in order that good works be meritorious of eternal life; still, even without sanctifying grace, we can do works which are good in the sight of God. God accepted the alms of the Centurion, who was an infidel, and Daniel counselled

Nabuchodonosor to give alms, etc. Hence sinners should endeavour to do good works, which, although they cannot *merit* for them eternal life, may yet serve to *impetrate* for them the mercy of God.

Some say that all the works of infidels and sinners are sins?

A. This detestable error was condemned in the twenty-fifth and thirty-fifth propositions of Baius by the Sovereign Pontiffs St. Pius V., Gregory XIII., and Urban VIII. I call it a detestable error, because it casts sinners into despair, and deprives them of the use of those means—that is to say, of good works—whereby they might obtain God's mercy and the grace of conversion.

Is sanctifying grace the same thing as charity?

A. The most probable opinion is, that it is the same thing; others, however, suppose it to be a gift distinct from charity. However this may be, it is certain that he who has charity has sanctifying grace, and he who has sanctifying grace has also charity.

Sect. III. *The Merit of Good Works.*

Are good works meritorious?

A. It is a truth of the Faith, defined by the Holy Council of Trent, that by good works, done in a state of grace, we truly merit an increase of the same grace, that is, of sanctifying grace and eternal life.

Now is it possible that by good works, which,

however many and great they may be, can bear no proportion to the pricelessness of an eternal reward, we can truly merit Paradise?

A. You must consider that by our good works, regarded in themselves alone, we could not merit eternal life, because there would be no proportion between these works and the reward which is given them. But we must look upon our good works as ennobled by the infinite merits of Jesus Christ, and raised to so great a dignity and value by His merits, that there is a most true proportion between them and eternal life. Further, we must pre-suppose the Divine promise, whereby God has bound Himself to reward them in this manner; the Divine promise which, in a wide sense, obliges Almighty God, in regard of us, to recompense us with this reward. I say in a *wide* sense, because God cannot be bound, in regard of us, by a rigorous debt, but He is bound by His own infinite fidelity which demands that He fail not in His promises. And so you see that Eternal Life is a true grace, inasmuch as all our merits spring from the grace of God; and it is by a simple act of His Divine Goodness that our good works are raised to so great a value as to merit Paradise, which also was promised to them by a simple act of His Divine Goodness. Paradise is, moreover, at the same time a true reward, because in virtue of the supernatural excellence and dignity of our good works, and in virtue of the Divine promise whereby God has bound Himself to reward them, this reward is truly due to them. Therefore, as is defined against the heretics, by good works performed in a state of grace, we truly merit, not only increase of the same grace, but also Eternal Life.

What conditions must good works have in order that they may be meritorious?

A. The first condition is, that the good works be done by men who are *wayfarers*, that is to say, during this life; for the Saints in Heaven, who are no longer wayfarers, but have finished their journey and attained their end, can no longer merit. The second is that they be *free;* for, in order to merit, it is necessary that a man know what he does, and that he can do or not do, what he does. The third condition is that they be done by a *just* man, that is, by one in a state of grace, as we have already shewn. The fourth is, that they be *good* works, good by a supernatural goodness, either in themselves, such as the receiving of the holy sacraments, or by reason of their end, such as the making a pilgrimage to some sanctuary in order to venerate a devout image of the Blessed Virgin. Those four conditions, besides the Divine Promise, which we take for granted, are the conditions which necessarily and undoubtedly are required in all good works, in order that they may be truly meritorious. This is the teaching of all Theologians.

For what reason does the Council say that increase of grace may be merited?

A. Because, as the same Council defines, the first sanctifying grace cannot be truly merited. The sinner, who is deprived of grace, may impetrate it by his prayers and good works, but truly merit it he cannot, his prayers and good works not being of sufficient value to do so. When, however, he obtains sanctifying grace, and is therefore justified, then by the good works which he thereafter performs, he truly merits the increase of this grace.

Explain to me more clearly the second condition, which requires that good works be *free.*

A. *Freedom* is essential in man, in order to his merits or demerits before God, that is, in the performing good works which shall be worthy of recompense, as well as in the committing sins which shall be worthy of punishment; and this freedom demands knowledge, and determination, not forced or necessitated by any cause, whether external or internal. It demands *knowledge;* and so if I bestow a gift on a poor man, believing him to be rich, my gift has not the merit of an alms ; in like manner, were I to give poison to some one, believing that I was giving him a wholesome drink, I should not incur the guilt of murder. It requires *determination,* without compulsion from any external cause ; therefore, for example, should any one by main force compel me to prostrate myself before the Blessed Sacrament, I should not have the merit of that adoration ; and if I were forced to prostrate myself before. an idol, I should not incur the guilt of idolatry. It is necessary, moreover, that there be no violence or compulsion proceeding from any internal cause; and therefore were the grace of God to force our will, as Calvin imagined, or draw it irresistibly, as Jansenius taught, there could be no merit in good works ; so likewise, if concupiscence forced or irresistibly drew our will, there would be no demerit in wicked works. And in truth ought we to suppose that possible in God, which we could not suppose possible in men, without doing them grievous wrong ? If a Sovereign were to reward good actions performed by one who could do no less than perform them, and to punish wicked actions committed by one who could do no other than commit them, should we not say that in the first case he was a fool, in the second that he was a tyrant ? From this you will easily understand why we say that for a man to merit, by his good works, it is necessary that he should know what he is doing, and that it should be in his power to do, or not to do, what he does. That free will remained to man after original sin, is a truth of the Faith defined by the Holy Council of Trent. Perfect freedom, exempt not only from all violence, but also from all necessity, in order to man's merits or demerits, is a truth of the Faith, as defined in the condemnation of the third proposition of Jansenius. Before Jansenius, Baius had blasphemously maintained that "man sins and merits punishment, even in those things which he does of necessity."

CHAPTER VI.

THE THEOLOGICAL VIRTUES.

SECT. I. *Explanation of the Theological Virtues;—
in general.*

How many Theological Virtues are there?

A. There are three, Faith, Hope, and Charity.

Why are they called Theological?

A. Because God is the object of these virtues.
By Faith we believe God, and we believe in God.
By Hope, we hope for God, that is for the possession of Him in Paradise; and we hope in God,
that is, in His aid. By Charity we love God, and
we also love our neighbour for God, that is, for the
love of God.

Are these Virtues supernatural?

A. They are supernatural; and this means that
by our natural strength we could not acquire them,
but God infuses them into our souls when we receive
Holy Baptism.

Do you mean to say then that children just baptized possess these Virtues; and are we also to
affirm that, before the use of reason, such children
believe, hope, and love?

A. It is certain that children, who are just baptized, do possess these Virtues; that is to say, they
have the habits of them, but they do not exercise
them by actually believing, hoping, and loving, because they are hindered from doing so by not having
the use of reason. We say they have the *habits* of

them, meaning thereby a prompt disposition actually to believe, to hope, and to love when they attain the use of reason. I will explain this by a comparison. A child, to whom his father at his death has left great wealth, is, in point of fact, rich whilst he is under the care of guardians, but he cannot dispose of his riches, he cannot spend them till the appointed time. So, before the use of reason, children have the habits of the Theological Virtues, but cannot then exercise them.

By making Acts of Faith, Hope, and Charity, do these Virtues grow in us?

A. By exercising the acts of any virtue whatsoever, virtues grow in us and attain greater perfection; and so the oftener we make Acts of Faith, the more lively will our Faith become; the more frequently we make Acts of Hope, the firmer will our Hope be; and the more we multiply Acts of Charity, the more ardent will be our Love.

Can these Virtues be lost?

A. Faith is lost by the sin of infidelity, which is committed when any one. does not will to believe, or advertently doubts some truth taught by Holy Church; for instance, he who would not believe, or should doubt, that there are seven Sacraments, would lose it. Hope is lost when one despairs of the Divine Mercy, that is, if he should think that God will no more pardon his sins. Charity is lost by any mortal sin whatever; therefore if we lose Faith or Hope, we also always lose Charity.

If these Virtues are lost, can they be regained?

A. They can be regained by due repentance of the sin which caused their loss.

Have the Saints in Heaven the Theological Virtues?

A. The Saints have Charity only; for, as is clear, all that they believed they now see in God, and what is an object of sight is no longer an object of Faith. What they formerly hoped for they now possess, since they enjoy God; and what is actually obtained is no longer an object of Hope. Faith and Hope, therefore, must accompany us to Paradise, but they will not enter with us.

Is there an obligation to make Acts of Faith, Hope, and Charity?

A. There is an express obligation to do so, as might be proved by numberless testimonies of Holy Scripture and of the Holy Fathers. The contrary error was condemned by Alexander VII. Therefore make these Acts frequently, and more particularly make frequent Acts of Charity.

SECT. II. *The Virtue of Faith.*

What is the Virtue of Faith?

A. It is a Theological Virtue infused by God into our souls, by which we firmly believe, from the motive of the Divine veracity, all those things which God has revealed, and which the Church proposes to be believed.

Why do you say *from the motive of the Divine Veracity?*

A. Because we firmly believe all those things which Holy Church proposes to us to believe, on the ground that God who has revealed them is Infallible Truth, and can neither deceive nor be deceived. The certainty of our Faith rests, therefore, on the Divine Veracity.

Why do you say all those things which God has revealed?

A. Because he who should fail to believe even one, would be an infidel; and as much wrong is done to Infinite Truth by doubting Its veracity on one point as on many.

Why do you say that the Church proposes them to us to believe?

A. Because God revealed truths immediately to the inspired writers, such as Moses, David, &c. In like manner truths were revealed by Christ to His Apostles; but now we cannot expect particular revelations as the Protestants do, who pretend that the Holy Spirit manifests directly to the understanding of each individual the truths which he is to believe. On the contrary, there is the Catholic Church who is the supreme Mistress of the Truth, and teaches infallibly to her children all those truths which they are to believe. She speaks by means of General Councils, and by means of the definitions of the Sovereign Pontiffs. For example, she taught, by means of the Holy Council of Trent, in opposition to the errors of the Protestants, that there are seven Sacraments. She taught, by means of definitions of the Supreme Pontiffs, in opposition to the errors of the Jansenists, that Christ did not die only for the elect : and he who should say that there are not seven Sacraments, would be as much a heretic as he who should say that Christ died on the Cross only for the predestinate. (See Sect. iii. of the chapter on the Sources of Theology.)

When can we give the name of Heretic to any one ?

A. When he pertinaciously asserts an error which is contrary to some truth of the Faith. I say *pertinaciously*, because if any one asserts an error out of ignorance, even culpable ignorance, he is not to be called a heretic. For example, a man neglecting to instruct himself, may not know that the Church has defined that there are seven Sacraments ; if he says that there are only three, he says what is heresy, but he is not a heretic, because he utters this heresy from ignorance.

In what respect does Heresy differ from Infidelity?

A. In this, that Infidelity is the privation or lack of Faith, in one who has never embraced it ; and in this way Idolaters, Turks and Jews, are infidels ; Heresy, on the contrary, is lack of Faith in one who has once embraced it as a baptized person, or at least as a catechumen. Further, heresy is a partial want of Faith, that is to say, when one or more dogmas, and not all, are disbelieved ; because if any one should deny all the dogmas of the Faith, and so absolutely renounce the Christian Religion, his sin would be *Apostacy.* A Christian, therefore, who should renounce his belief in Christ and in His Church, to become a Turk, would not be called a heretic, but an apostate. This is meant, speaking with the precision of the schools, because the name of infidels can be given even to heretics, inasmuch as, sinning against the Faith, they lose the virtue of Faith. The sin, therefore, of not believing, or of doubting any article of the Faith, is called the sin of Infidelity.

How many kinds of Infidelity are there, properly so called ?

A. There are two kinds, negative infidelity and positive infidelity. *Negative* Infidelity is found in those who do not believe, because they have never heard, and never could have heard, the truths of the Faith announced to them ; and this is not sin. *Positive* Infidelity is found in those who have heard the truths of the Faith preached to them and will not believe, or who might have heard them preached and would not give ear to them ; and this is sin.

Will infidels who have never heard the truths of Faith announced to them, and who have never had the opportunity of hearing them, be saved?

A. Without Faith it is impossible that any one should be saved, for St. Paul says that without Faith it is impossible to please God. (Heb. xi.) . Nevertheless if those infidels should observe the natural law, the Lord would supply their necessity either by ordinary or by extraordinary means, even sending an Angel to instruct them, were it necessary, as St. Thomas says, and as we have already shewn. If those infidels sin against the natural law, they are damned for such sins, and not for the sin of infidelity, which in them is not voluntary.

How many kinds of Acts of Faith are there? ·

A. There are two kinds, Internal and External.

How do you define an Internal Act of Faith?

A. It is the firm consent of our mind to believe revealed truths.

How is an Internal Act of Faith subdivided?

A. Into implicit and explicit. It is an Implicit Act of Faith when, without regard had to one dogma more than to another, we believe generally all that the Holy Catholic Church teaches: it is Explicit when we believe expressly one or more determinate articles of the Faith. For example, if I say,—I firmly believe all the truths which the Church teaches; or if, not knowing what the Holy Council of Trent has defined concerning the doctrine of justification, I say: In regard to justification,—I believe all that the Church teaches, it is an *Implicit* Act of Faith. But if, on the other hand, I say,—I believe that there are seven Sacraments; or,—I believe that, without the grace of God, I can do nothing that shall avail for Eternal Life,—it is an *Explicit* Act of Faith.

Is Implicit Faith sufficient for salvation, that is to

say, does it suffice to believe all that the Church teaches, without knowing what she teaches?

A. This Faith does not suffice, because it is necessary to believe explicitly the principal truths of our Holy Religion, that is, we must know them. The principal truths are, that God is Just, and therefore that He rewards the good and punishes the wicked; that God is One in Three Persons, that is to say, the mystery of the Blessed Trinity; that the Second Person of the Blessed Trinity, that is, the Son, was made Man, and as Man suffered and died for our salvation : whoever does not believe these truths expressly, is not capable of receiving the Holy Sacraments, and cannot be saved. Moreover we must believe expressly all the other truths which are in the Apostles' Creed ; though any one who should not know them without fault on his part, that is to say, because he was not able to learn them, might be saved. The first must be known by necessity of *means;* the second by necessity of *precept.* In regard to many other truths which Holy Church has defined, it is not necessary that all Christians should know them, but each one must instruct himself according to his own state and capacity. We must resort to instructions, and if we cannot attain to a distinct knowledge of some articles of the Faith, it will suffice that we believe them implicitly, intending to believe all that Holy Church teaches. Observe also, by the way, that besides the Creed, it is necessary to know the Pater Noster, the Ave Maria, the Commandments of the Law of God, and of the Church, all that is necessary for the worthy reception of those Sacraments, to which we must approach, and the duties of our own state.

During the time of the Law of Nature, that is, before God gave the Written Law to Moses, and during the time of this written law, until the coming of our Saviour, what Faith was necessary for men in order that they might obtain Eternal Life ?

A. Besides believing that God punishes the wicked and rewards the good, it was necessary for them to have an *implicit* Faith in the Saviour of the world ; that is to say, to have some knowledge of the promised Saviour. And so all the Just of the Old Testament were saved, not only through the merits of Jesus Christ, but through Faith in the same Christ.

When are we obliged to make Internal Acts of Faith ?

A. I have already shewn that we ought to make them frequently, and in particular at the commencement of the use of reason, and at the hour of death. Some have said that it suffices to make one single Act of Faith during our whole life, but this mistake was condemned by the Holy Pontiff Innocent XI.

I should like to know whether an Internal Act of Faith can consist with doubt of the truth of the things believed ?

A. In defining Faith, we have said that it is a

virtue by which we believe firmly, therefore it cannot consist with doubt of the truth of the things believed. Faith excludes all doubt, and includes certainty that the thing cannot be otherwise.

What can we say then of certain Catholics, who, listening to errors against the Faith, as for example, against the eternity of the pains of Hell, against Purgatory, against the Virginity of the Blessed Virgin Mary, against the Supremacy of the Pope, profess themselves Catholics, but still think that the Protestants who teach these errors may probably, or at least possibly, be right?

A. If they admit doubt, that is to say, if they admit the probability, or even the possibility, that the Church may err in teaching the contrary truths, they have lost the Faith, and if they profess still to be Catholics, they profess to be what they are not. He who does not believe firmly, absolutely, does not believe with that Divine Faith which is necessary for salvation.

A Catholic Christian, however, may examine if the things which the Church teaches him are really true?

A. If a Catholic Christian examines the truths which the Church teaches him, in order to know if they are really true, and therefore doubts whether they may not be false, he shows by so doing that he has already lost the Faith, which is destroyed in every case whatsoever, by every doubt, if such doubt be adverted and consented to.

But then we must believe without reason, or even against reason, however unanswerable may be the arguments against those things which the Church teaches?

A. There is no doubt that we must believe under any circumstances; because if Divine Faith, from any motive, ceases to be firm and unshaken, by that very fact it is destroyed. Besides, Divine Faith can never be without, or against reason, for it rests on the infallible authority of God revealing; and if the things which Holy Church teaches appear to us to be without reason, or contrary to reason, this proceeds from our ignorance, and limited understanding, which cannot arrive at comprehension of the truth of the Divine Mysteries; just as many physical and mathematical truths which are evident to philosophers, appear to an ignorant man to be without reason, or contrary to reason. We must be firmly persuaded that whatever argument we may find against truths revealed by God, however strange and unanswerable it may seem to be, can only be a false reason and a sophism.

And yet we exhort Protestants and other unbelievers to examine the truths which the Faith teaches, in order that they may be convinced in regard to them. Now if they may examine them, why may not we also examine them?

A. Observe the difference there is between them and us Catholics. They have not as yet Divine Faith,

and therefore cannot lose it by doubt, and it is needful that by study they should convince themselves
of the truth, and dispose themselves to obtain this
gift from God; we, on the contrary, have this gift
already, hence, whilst we cannot acquire it, we
might lose it by admitting doubt. Nevertheless we
may examine the truths of the Faith, in order the
better to know their reasonableness, and to put ourselves in a position to convince others. We must
make this examination, however, with firm belief,
without admitting even the shadow of a doubt.

Why do you say that Protestants have not Divine
Faith? They believe many revealed truths as well
as we do, therefore, in regard to those truths, have
they not the faith that we have?

A. Divine Faith is a supernatural gift, which only
those who are members of Holy Church can possess; therefore Protestants, who are outside the
Church, are deprived of this gift, and if they believe
some truths of the Faith, they believe them with
human faith, that is to say, from the conviction
produced in their minds, by the reasons which militate in favour of these truths. For example, we
believe that Christ is the Saviour, and that Plato
was a philosopher; we believe the first of those
truths by a virtue, or supernatural force, which
operates on our minds, and inclines us to believe it;
we believe the second, by force of the arguments
with which history presents us; and so we believe
the first with *Divine* faith, the second with *human*

faith. Protestants who believe both these truths with us, believe both by the power exercised on their minds by the reasons which militate in favour of both the one and the other, without that super-natural aid which inclines us Catholics to believe the first ; therefore, when they believe that Christ is the Saviour, they believe it, not with *Divine Faith* but with *mere Human Faith.*

When do we make an External Act of Faith ?

A. When we manifest our Internal Faith in a visible or sensible manner. If I say that I am a Christian, if I prostrate myself before the Blessed Sacrament, &c.,—these are External Acts of Faith.

Is it necessary to make External Acts of Faith ?

A. It is most necessary, and St. Paul says so expressly (Romans x.); therefore it is not enough to have Faith only in our heads, we must manifest it in our words and actions.

But when, by manifesting our Faith, we might be threatened with some grave injury, might we not feign that we are not Christians, or might we not out-wardly renounce our Faith, retaining it in our hearts?

A. This would be a very great sin. Like the Holy Martyrs, we should be ready to suffer any kind of death, rather than renounce our Holy Faith, or feign not to be Christians.

But will not God, who sees the heart, be content with the homage of the heart, particularly if we could not manifest our Faith without serious injury ?

A. God, who is Sovereign Lord of the whole

man, which consists of soul and body, requires, by every right, the homage of the whole man, that is both internal and spiritual homage, and external and material homage. To disguise and hide our Faith, in order to make men believe that we are without it, or to make pretence of renouncing our Faith, is abominable cowardice and ingratitude towards God, whose gift it is. He made himself Man, and sacrificed His infinitely precious life for us ; is it not just then that we should shew ourselves ready to sacrifice our lives, which are of so little value, for His honour? Moreover, if He permits our Faith to be tempted, He gives us powerful aid to resist every trial. Therefore, however serious may be the consequences, we must, when needful, after the example of the Holy Martyrs, manifest our Faith to the world.

In theology, are those things only certain which the Church has already defined, and declared to be of Faith ?

A. It would be a grave error to say that those things only are certain, which the Church has already defined, and declared to be of faith, which is easily proved if you only consider the definition of the dogma of the Immaculate Conception of the Blessed Virgin Mary. In point of fact, this truth was not a defined dogma, and declared to be of faith before the 8th of December of the year 1854; nevertheless it was a most certain truth, a truth such that the Church had threatened with excommunication not only whoever should deny it in express terms, but also any one who should dare to allege any objections against it, without at the same time confuting them by sufficient arguments.

It does not follow that, because a truth has not been defined and declared to be of faith, it may be denied with impunity, or at least looked upon as doubtful, but only that he who does not believe it, or doubts it, is not guilty of the sin of *heresy*, though he may be guilty of the most grievous rashness. Before the Council of Trent, certain truths were not defined and declared to be of faith, which in that Council were defined and declared to be so, against the novelties of the Protestants; and yet those truths were commonly believed, and recognized as certain by Holy Church, and it would have been grave temerity to deny or cast doubt upon them, as Luther and Calvin did.

If it were necessary that a truth should be defined and declared to be of faith, in order to be certain, it would not be certain that Christ walked upon earth with His Feet, such fact having never been defined and declared to be of faith.

Hence we clearly perceive that it would be a perverse and unreasonable mode of reasoning for a theologian to argue thus,—it is not defined and declared to be of faith, that in Hell there is material fire,—that the Diaconate is a sacrament,—that the contracting parties are the ministers of the sacrament of matrimony,—that the Pope is infallible when he speaks *ex cathedra,* and is superior to a General Council ;* therefore all these things may be denied, or regarded as doubtful. A theologian who should reason in this manner, would err grievously, for although these truths have not been defined and declared as of faith, they are commonly believed, and recognized as certain by the Church.

Sect. II. *The Virtue of Hope.*

What is the Virtue of Hope ?

A. It is a Theological Virtue, by which, with certain confidence, we expect Eternal Happiness and the means to attain thereto, through the Divine aid, and according to the promise which God has made us in regard of the merits of Jesus Christ.

Why do you say *with certain confidence?*

A. Because our hope rests on the infinite merits of Jesus Christ, and on His promise that He will give us Paradise in reward for our good works, and that He will give us the necessary means to attain it, therefore our hope is certain and secure. Hence St. Paul calls it,—an anchor of the soul, sure and firm (Heb. vi. 19.).

You mean to say then that we cannot fear being lost ?

A. Observe that I say *certain confidence,* and not *sure certainty;* because confidence of attaining

* This cannot now, since the date of the Vatican Council, be adduced as an example. See p. 30.—ED.

any good always pre-supposes the peril of losing it.
Now on God's part our hope is most certain,
because nothing that is necessary for our salvation
can be wanting to us on His part; but on our part
the necessary correspondence to His grace may be
wanting, and therefore we cannot say that we are
certain that we shall infallibly be saved. Looking
therefore at the certainty of the Divine Promise on
the one side, and at our weakness on the other, our
Hope cannot be an *absolute certainty*, but only a
certain confidence.

Ought we, in short, to feel most confidence in regard
to the certainty there is on God's part, or most fear in
regard to the danger arising from our own weakness?

A. We ought to feel most confidence in regard
to the certainty there is on God's part, because the
goodness of God is infinitely greater than our
wickedness; therefore our confidence in God ought
to be greater than our fear of ourselves.

Can, then, the fear of Hell subsist with the hope
of Paradise?

A. You must distinguish between different kinds
of fear. There is the fear called *Filial Fear*, whereby
we fear Hell, as we fear an offence against God,
which alone can confine souls in Hell, and we fear
it as an injury done to Infinite Goodness; such
fear is not fear of our own injury, as it is our own
injury, but fear of injury to the object beloved,
that is to God. Again, there is the fear called
Servile Fear, whereby we fear Hell as an injury to

ourselves, but without affection to sin, by which we
merit Hell.   Again there is the fear called *Servilely
Servile Fear*, with which we fear Hell on account of
the injury to ourselves, but *with affection to sin*, so
that it is not sin, but Hell which displeases us, and
we would wish, in a way, that there were no Hell, in
order to be able to sin without fear.   The first, as is
clearly evident, is a most holy fear; the second
also is good, as the Holy Council of Trent defined
against the heretics; so that both the first and
second kinds of fear can well subsist with Christian
Hope.   The third kind is the fear of the wicked,
and most unworthy of Christians.

Is it not an interested and defective service to
serve God, with the hope of reward?

A. Some false mystics of these later times have
thought so, but their errors have been condemned
by the Sovereign Pontiffs.   The Holy Spirit, as we
learn from the Scriptures, would have us hope for
Paradise, and this hope has animated the greatest
Saints to do great things for God; hence, when we
serve our Lord, hoping that He will recompense our
service with an eternal reward, we do not commit
any defect, but exercise the most necessary virtue
of Hope.   Observe that the Council of Trent excommunicated anyone who should say that the just
sin, when they perform good works in order to gain
an eternal reward.

Can we say, then, that sinners commit sin, when
they perform works in order to gain this reward?

A. If sinners should perform good works in order to gain Paradise, but with the intention of not being converted to God, they would most certainly commit sin ; because it is the worst kind of presumption to expect salvation without having the will to forsake sin ; but, if sinners perform good works in order to attain God's mercy, to reconcile themselves to Him, and hence to attain salvation, they do that which is good and holy ; in fact this is what God commands, and what He would have them do.

Ought we to hope for Paradise, only for our own good ?

A. We ought to refer all our good to God, and therefore we ought to hope for, and to seek the blessedness of Heaven, in order that it may redound to the Eternal Glory of God. In one word, we ought to endeavour to become Saints, in order that God may be glorified by our sanctity. This is taken from the Holy Council of Trent.*

You said a little while ago that our Hope rests on the infinite merits of Jesus Christ : what do you mean by that ?

A. Jesus Christ is our Saviour : He offered the infinite merits of His Incarnation, Passion, and

---

* The Council declares those to be heretics, who hold that in all their works the just sin, if in them they excite their indolences and are moved to running the race, by this, that in the first place God be glorified, but also in view of an eternal reward.

Death for us ; and by the value of His merits we have been made capable of meriting Heaven.

You added that our Hope rests on the promise of God to give us Heaven in reward of our good works : what do you mean by that?

A. We have seen in Sect. 3, Chap. 5, that we could not merit Heaven without that promise ; therefore all our hope rests on it. This Divine promise is the motive through which we hope for Heaven.

When we exercise Acts of Hope, must we have the intention of performing good works?

A. Without such intention our hope would become presumption, because Heaven is promised to the merit of good works ; and we can only have a solid foundation for our Hope of salvation, when we have the intention to do the good that is required of us in order to attain thereto.

SECT. III.   *The Virtue of Charity.*

What is the Virtue of Charity?

A. It is a Theological Virtue, infused by God into our souls, by which we love God above all things, because He is the Infinite Good, and love our neighbour for the love of God.

What do you mean by saying that we love God because He is the Infinite Good?

A. God ought to be loved for His Infinite Goodness. Everything is loved in proportion to the goodness contained in it; therefore we love a thing because it is good, and, the better it is, the more we love it. Hence we love God because He is good, and we love Him above all things, because there is no goodness which can be put in comparison with His.

In how many ways can we love God above all things?

A. In two ways, *appreciatively* and *intensely*. God is loved above all things *appreciatively* when the will is so united to God that it is ready to suffer anything whatever, rather than offend Him by any mortal sin; He is loved *intensely*, above all things, when, to the firmness and attachment of the will, is united a lively transport and ardent affection, so that nothing makes so great impression on the feelings of our heart, as the pleasure or displeasure of Almighty God.

In which of these two ways are we obliged to love God?

A. In the first, that is to say, *appreciatively*; and he who should be without this love could not be saved.

Does this *appreciative* love oblige us only to abstain from mortal sin?

A. Appreciative love obliges us to prefer Almighty God and His good pleasure before all things, and therefore to abstain even from venial sin; nevertheless, since venial sin does not extinguish charity in us, appreciative love would suffice for our salvation, although it might not attain to making us avoid venial sin.

For what reason are we not obliged to love God *intensely* above all things?

A. Because this intense love is not in our own power; it is an extraordinary gift of .God, most precious and greatly to be desired. The purest souls possess it, generally speaking, even in this life; still, even they have not the fulness of the intensity of the Divine love, this fulness of love being reserved for the Saints in Heaven.

How can it be that a soul should prefer God and His good pleasure before all things, whilst some other object may make greater impression on the feelings of the heart?

A. The *act* of giving preference to one thing before all others is an act of the *will*, which is free; *feeling* the impression of one thing more than another belongs to the *sensitive* faculty, which in us is not free, but of necessity. For example, I may determine to give preference to bitter food instead of sweet, but I cannot prevent myself *feeling* the bitterness when I eat it. From the same sensitive faculty it arises that even pious mothers feel more lively joy in seeing their children restored to health after a dangerous illness, than in seeing them penitent after the commission of some sin; and yet their *will* would prefer rather to see them sick than sinners.

When a man prefers God before all things be-

cause He is an infinite good, and would lose anything whatever rather than offend Him grievously,
has he the perfect love of God?

A. It is certain that such an one then possesses
the perfect love of God; perfect in its nature, though
capable of becoming more and more perfect, as is
clearly seen in the case of a man who would be
ready to lose anything whatever rather than offend
God by even a venial sin.

Can Love, or perfect Charity subsist in a soul
together with mortal sin?

A. Baius taught that perfect Charity might be
found in a soul together with mortal sin, but the
Church has condemned this doctrine. Hence it is
certain that the perfect love of God cannot be found
in any soul together with mortal sin, any more than
light can be in a room at the same time with darkness.

But suppose the case, that a person guilty of
some mortal sin should make an act of perfect love
of God, should we not then find in the same soul
mortal sin and the perfect love of God?

A. This could never happen, because that act of
perfect love of God would immediately expel mortal
sin from the soul, just as a lighted taper when carried
into a dark room at once expels the darkness.

But is not Sacramental Confession required, in
order to take away sin from the soul?

A. Sacramental Confession is requisite, either in
effect or in intention. It is requisite in effect, when

there is only Attrition; and in that case it is necessary for a Christian to confess, and receive Sacramental Absolution, in order to expel sin from his soul. But when there is perfect Charity, then the intention to confess at the usual time suffices. He who has Charity or the perfect Love of God, has Contrition *implicitly*, that is to say, sorrow for having offended God, it being impossible that any one should love God above all things, and not abhor sin above all things; he has also the intention of confessing at the usual time, because it is equally impossible that any one should love God above all things, and not have the intention of obeying His commands; therefore, if a sinner makes an act of perfect love of God he is immediately justified. Nevertheless, he is obliged to confess his mortal sins at the proper time, that is to say, when he has to fulfil the precept of Confession, or, even when he does confess, apart from precept, as is clearly to be understood.

Might we not say that the perfect love of God justifies the soul only in case of necessity, as, for instance, when at the point of death it is not possible to have a Confessor?

A. He who should say this, would in effect say that perfect charity may subsist in the soul together with mortal sin, and would assert a proposition precisely condemned in Baius.* If charity is

---

* This is the proposition of Baius. "By contrition, even with perfect charity, and with a desire of receiving the

perfect, that is to say, if God is loved above all things, because He is an infinite good, mortal sin is immediately taken away from the soul.

Suppose a man to have been justified by some act of perfect love of God, including the intention of confession at a convenient time ; if such an one should change his intention, and resolve never to go to confession again, would the mortal sins, which were cancelled by his act of the love of God, return once more to stain his soul ?

A. It is a most certain truth, that sins which have been once cancelled cannot again return to stain the soul : other similar sins may be committed, but the same sins cannot return again. Take the following comparison : You drop a pocket-handkerchief in the mud, so that it is dirty and stained ; you rinse it out in a stream, and the stains and dirt are washed out by the water ; that dirt, those particular stains are removed, they are gone with the stream, and it is impossible that the handkerchief can be stained by them any more, although it might be stained anew, should you again let it fall in the mud. Observe, however, that a person who should have the evil intention of going no more to Confession, would commit a fresh mortal sin, and would immediately lose the love of God, and His grace.

---

sacrament, sin is not remitted, save in case of necessity, or of martyrdom, without actual reception of the sacrament."

If the perfect love of God has so great an efficacy, as to restore the soul to a state of grace, even beyond the case of necessity, a person in mortal sin need not think it of great consequence to confess his sin at once, but may rest satisfied with making acts of the love of God, and acts of contrition.

A. Beware of drawing such a conclusion, for it is false. Not all who make acts of the love of God and acts of contrition, make them with that perfection which is requisite in order that they may take away sin from the soul, and therefore many persons might believe themselves to be justified, whilst they were really in mortal sin. Moreover, although the acts of the love of God and the acts of contrition might be perfect, they would not confer *Sacramental* grace, which is given solely in the Sacrament of Penance when the penitent receives absolution. Hence the soul would remain without the great help of this grace, of which we shall speak in the 15th Answer of the 1st. §, Chapter vii. Therefore, when one falls into mortal sin, let him immediately make acts of contrition, in order that by making one perfectly he may speedily recover the grace of God; but then, without waiting for the obligation of annual confession, or even for his own convenience, let him go as soon as he can to confession, in order to provide for his soul in the best way possible in a matter of so great importance. The doctrine of the efficacy and value of contrition must be taught, because it is the doctrine of the Church, and because every one ought to know the value of the Virtue of Charity and of Acts of Charity; but no one must take occasion from this doctrine to defer going to confession after having committed mortal sin. However great may be the contrition which he feels in his heart, let the sinner go to confession as soon as he can, even if it be to his own inconvenience.

How ought we to love our neighbour?

A. We ought to love him as we love ourselves, and for the love of God. Thus the love of our neighbour is founded in the love of God, inasmuch as we love our neighbour in regard of God, and for the love we bear to God.

If a man love his neighbour because he is of a good disposition, because he is learned, rich, his benefactor, his friend, or his relation, does he love him with the love of charity?

A. If he love him for these titles and reasons only, he loves him with a *natural* love, which is found even in infidels, and therefore does not love him with *supernatural* love, such as the love of charity is; besides all these motives, then, he must love him also for the love of God, and because God wills that he should love Him.

Must we love all our neighbours, absolutely and without distinction?

A. We must love all our neighbours absolutely, whether friends or enemies, good or bad, faithful or unfaithful to us; nevertheless there may be distinctions in our love, seeing we ought to prefer our friends and relations, our benefactors, those who are faithful, &c., to those who are not so. Thus, for example, if we had to clothe two poor persons, one of whom was a relation, and the other not, and we had but one coat to give away, we ought to give it to our relation.

In order to love our neighbour, does it not suffice to do him good, without however loving him in our heart?

A. It does not suffice; and Pope Innocent XI. condemned two propositions which said that we are not bound to love our neighbour with internal and formal acts, but that we can satisfy the precept by mere external acts. Therefore, it is necessary to love our neighbour with affection of the heart, and hence to do to him what we would reasonably wish done to us, and not to do to him what we would not reasonably have done to us.

Are we obliged to make Acts of Charity, equally with Acts of Faith and Hope?

A. We are; and Theologians agree that we are even obliged to make them more frequently.

Does the precept of charity oblige us to refer all our actions to the service and glory of God?

A. Certainly; it obliges us to refer to the glory of God and to His service all our actions, even such indifferent actions as eating, sleeping, suitable amusements, recreations, &c.

Is it necessary in every action that we perform, to say expressly : I intend to do this for the glory of God ?

A. This is not necessary ; it suffices that, from time to time, we renew our intention of doing all our actions for the glory of God.

CHAPTER VII.

THE SACRAMENTS.

SECT. I.   *The Sacraments;—in general.*

How do you define the word Sacrament ?

A. A Sacrament is a sacred sign, (visible and permanent; instituted by Christ, which effects, *ex opere operato*, our sanctification.   This definition belongs to all the Sacraments of the New Law, that is to say, to all the Sacraments of the Church.

Are there then other Sacraments besides those of the New Law ?

A. Before Christ instituted the Sacraments which are administered in the Church, that is to say, before His coming, there were Sacraments, but they were very inferior to ours, and such as it is not necessary to speak of in this compendium.   It is sufficient to observe that he who should say that the Sacraments of the Old Law were of equal value with the Sacraments of the New Law, that is to say, with the Sacraments of Holy Church, would be a eretic.   (Council of Trent.   Sess. 6.)

For what reason is the word *Sacrament* defined as—a *sign ?*

A. Because it makes known to us the thing which it signifies.   Thus, in Baptism, the washing makes known to us the purity which the soul acquires in receiving this sacrament.

Why is it called a *sacred* sign ?

A. Because the use of such a sign is a religious act pertaining to the worship of God.

Why is it called *visible?*

A. It is called *visible*, because it is necessary that it fall under the cognisance of the senses, that is to say, that in some way it should be material; therefore here the term visible is used in the signification of *sensible.* Anything purely spiritual could not be a sacrament.

Why is it called *permanent?*

A. Because the Sacraments are the foundations of Religion, and, like Religion, must endure perpetually; hence the Sacraments are rites which will continue even to the end of the world.

Why is a Sacrament said to be instituted by Jesus Christ?

A. Because He is the Author of all the Sacraments which are administered in the Church, as is defined by the Holy Council of Trent.

Why is it said, to effect our sanctification, *ex opere operato?*

A. Because the Sacraments have the intrinsic virtue of conferring grace on the soul, so that it is not the good dispositions which confer grace when we receive the Sacraments, but the Sacraments themselves which confer it. That they confer it *ex opere operato* is an article of the Faith, defined by the Holy Council of Trent.

It is of no importance then to approach the Sacraments with good dispositions?

A. It is of the utmost importance, and moreover necessary, in order that the Sacraments may produce their effect, in the same way that it is of importance and necessary that wood should be dry, in order that it may burn quickly. If you take dry wood and put it on the fire, it soon burns ; if you take wood full of spring sap, you will find it impossible to kindle it into a flame. (The property of burning, however, is neither in the dry nor in the green wood, the property of burning is in the fire) In like manner when the Sacraments are given to one who is well disposed for their reception, he acquires either grace or an augmentation of grace, because there exists no impediment to hinder their effect ; if, on the contrary, they are given to one who is not well disposed for their reception, he does not acquire grace, because there exists the impediment of his bad dispositions, which impediment does not suffer them to produce their effect, just as the quantity of moisture does not suffer the fire to burn the green wood. Therefore I repeat, that as the property of burning is in the fire, and not in the dispositions of the wood, so the property of conferring grace is in the Sacraments, and not in the dispositions of him who receives them.

Will not the effect of the Sacrament be greater or less, according to the greater or less disposition of him who receives it ?

A. Certainly it is so ; just as we see that the effect of fire is greater or less, according as the wood which is set on fire is more or less dry.

Why do you say that the Sacraments either *confer* or *increase* grace ?

A. Because some of the Sacraments are instituted in order to *confer* sanctifying grace on those
who lack it; and others to *increase* grace in
those who already possess it. ' Baptism and Penance
confer grace on those who do not possess it; all
the other Sacraments, on the contrary, increase grace
in those who have already received it, and preserved
it.' The first two are called Sacraments of the Dead,
and all the others, Sacraments of the Living; because
the first two are given to those who are dead to the
grace of God, and the others to those who are
alive by the same grace.

May there not be cases in which the Sacraments
of the Dead increase grace in those who already
possess it, and in which the Sacraments of the Living
confer grace on those who are deprived of it?

A. Such cases may certainly occur. Suppose
that a catechumen(by a perfect act of Contrition,
puts himself into a state of grace before he receives
Baptism, when he afterwards receives Baptism,
the sacrament cannot *confer* grace on him, but can
only *increase* it. The same may be said of the
Sacrament of Penance, when the penitent, by his
perfect contrition, is already in a state of grace
before he receives absolution; or, if he have only
venial sins to confess. In such cases, the Sacraments of the Dead *increase* sanctifying grace in
those who already possess it. All this is certain;
and there is no room for doubt in regard to it.
On the other hand, the Sacraments of the Living

sometimes confer sanctifying grace on those who are deprived of it, as theologians, with St. Thomas, commonly teach. Suppose a person with simple attrition, makes his confession to a priest who has not the necessary jurisdiction, or to a layman who pretends to be a priest. Such a person, in spite of his confession, remains in a state of mortal sin; but if, afterwards, believing himself to be validly absolved, he approaches to the Holy Table, then Holy Communion puts him in a state of grace, the Most Holy Eucharist, which is a Sacrament of the Living, conferring on him that grace which, as yet, he does not possess. What I say of the Most Holy Eucharist holds good in regard to all the other Sacraments of the Living, whenever, without fault on his own part, they are received by a person in a state of mortal sin, but who has repented of his mortal sin with the sorrow of attrition. The reason is, that attrition removes from the soul the evil will which would be an impediment to the acquisition of grace.

If this be so, we can always approach the Sacraments of the Living with simple attrition, without the necessity of confession. By attrition we shall remove the impediment of an evil will, and thus the Sacraments of the Living will confer on us sanctifying grace?

A. By no means; the Sacraments of the Living were not instituted by Jesus Christ in order that

of their institution they should *confer* sanctifying grace
on those who are deprived of it; but in order that
they should give *augmentation* of grace to those who
already possess it; and therefore there is an express
Divine command that men are not to approach
those sacraments, except in a state of grace. So
that he who knows himself to be still in mortal sin,
and yet chooses to approach them, transgresses
this Divine command, and, by so doing, commits a
fresh mortal sin : hence in him, the attrition would
be false, because it would be united to the will to
transgress a Divine command; and could not
remove the impediment to obtaining sanctifying
grace. Only, *per accidens*, as Theologians say, that
is to say, when a man is in good faith, and has done
all that he knows he ought to do in order to place
himself in the grace of God, when he believes himself to be justified and rightly disposed, so that if
he were conscious of having still the stain of sin
upon his soul, he would abstain from receiving this
or that Sacrament of the Living—in this case only,
and having, moreover, attrition for his mortal sins,
by receiving one of these sacraments, he obtains
sanctifying grace.

You mean to say then, that in order worthily to
receive the Sacraments of the Living, we must first
either confess our sins with attrition, or excite ourselves to perfect contrition ; and that one or other
of these, it matters not which, will suffice, since
both one and the other places us in a state of grace ?

A. If you mean that one or other of these indifferently suffices for all the Sacraments of the Living, you greatly err; for in order to receive the Most Holy Eucharist, it is not sufficient that those who are in mortal sin should make an act of contrition; they are under obligation, except in case of indispensable necessity, of going to Confession; the Sacred Council of Trent having thus understood the precept of St. Paul : *Probet autem seipsum homo,* "Let a man prove himself." In like manner those who are in mortal sin and find themselves at the point of death, should confess their sins, because presently they will be unable to satisfy the precept of confession; and so they could not receive Extreme Unction without Confession, and with merely making an act of Contrition. In regard, however, to Confirmation, Holy Orders, and Matrimony, there is no express command that Confession should precede them; it would suffice therefore, that those who are about to receive any one of these Sacraments should repent of their sins with true contrition, having, however, the intention of confessing in due time. Observe, nevertheless, that this doctrine is not to be preached to simple people; it is well that they should be ignorant of it, lest they should abuse it to their own injury, and with a mere imperfect act of contrition on the tip of their tongue, approach the Sacraments of Confirmation and Matrimony. You should know this doctrine, as a rule for yourselves, in order that you may not preach that there is equal necessity that Confession should precede Confirmation and Matrimony, as Communion, which would be false ; inasmuch as in regard to Communion there is the precept of St. Paul, which is not found in regard to the three foresaid sacraments. Preach, however, none the less, that the means left us by Jesus Christ to cleanse the soul from mortal sin is Sacramental Confession ; and that, therefore, every one who finds himself guilty of grievous sin, must go to confession before approaching to receive any sacrament whatsoever.

Do the Sacraments confer other graces, besides sanctifying grace ?

A. They each confer a grace *proper to the Sacrament*, to wit, a right founded on the sanctifying grace conferred by the sacrament, to receive at opportune times certain aids, or actual graces, in order that a man may obtain the end of the sacrament. Hence the *sacramental* grace of Baptism entitles one to seasonable aids to lead a life worthy of a Christian ; the *sacramental* grace of Confirmation gives one special aids to confess the Faith courageously ; that of the Eucharist, to nourish, that is, to preserve and increase charity ; that of Penance, to avoid sin for the future ; that of Extreme Unction, to make a good and tranquil passage to the other life ; that of Holy Orders, to comport oneself worthily and with zeal in the Sacred Ministry ; that of Matrimony, that the wedded may lead a peaceable life, and train up their children in the holy fear of God.

Who has given so great an efficacy to the Sacraments?

A. Jesus Christ, who is the Author of them, and who has merited it for them by the merits of His Incarnation, Passion, and Death.

Do the Sacraments produce any other effect, besides conferring *sanctifying*, and *sacramental* grace?

A. Three of the Sacraments, namely, Baptism, Confirmation, and Order, confer *character*, that is, a spiritual, indelible mark imprinted on the soul, by means of which those who shall have received all three, or any one of these sacraments, will be distinguished to all eternity from those who have not received them. This *character* will be for a special glory to the Blessed; and for a special confusion to the damned. Observe also that it is an article of the Faith that those three sacraments can be received but once.

Is it of Faith that this character will be indelible to all eternity?

A. It is certainly an article of the Faith, defined by the Council of Trent, that this character can never be cancelled during this life; but it is not a matter expressly defined as of Faith, that it shall be indelible also for all eternity. Such is, however, the teaching of St. Thomas, and the general sentiment of the Faithful.

Would one who should receive these three sacraments with bad dispositions, remain for ever deprived of the effects of those sacraments ?

A. When any one of these sacraments has been received validly, but bad dispositions have hindered the effect of the sacrament ; for instance, if one have received Baptism, with an affection to mortal sin, or Confirmation, or Order, in a state of mortal sin, Theologians say that if the bad dispositions be removed by a good confession, or, at least, by an act of contrition including the desire of confession, as has been already shewn (Ch. 6, § iv.), then the effect of these sacraments, however badly received, *revives*, so that the sacramental aids of which the man was deprived when he received these sacraments will be obtained. They teach the same in regard to Matrimony and Extreme Unction, because they suppose that the Divine Compassion will not suffer penitent sinners to be deprived of the special aids which the wedded need or the whole or nearly the whole of their lives, and which the dying need in order to make a good passage into eternity. The Sacraments however of Penance and the Eucharist, which may be received as often as we will, do not revive in their effects ; and those who have received them badly must repair the loss by receiving them well another time. If, however, a sacrament have been received, not only with bad dispositions, but *invalidly,* it is certain that it must be received anew ; and this even in the case of Baptism.

What things are required to the validity of the Sacraments?

A. Matter, form, a proper minister, and intention.

What is the *matter* in the Sacraments?

A. The matter is the thing used in conferring the Sacrament; for example, in Baptism, the matter is water.

What is the *form*?

A. The words which are uttered in conferring the Sacrament; for instance, in Baptism, the form is: I baptize thee, in the Name of the Father, and of the Son, and of the Holy Ghost.

Can the Church change the matter or form of the Sacraments?

A. The Church, as the Sacred Council of Trent teaches, has no authority to change the matter or form of the Sacraments; hence, if the matter or form were changed, the Sacraments would be valueless.

Still, in different places there is some difference in the form of the Sacraments?

A. There are accidental differences in words, which do not substantially change the meaning. If in any place a form were used which changed the sense of the form instituted by Christ, the sacrament would be without effect, and the Church would not permit it.

Who is the *Minister* of the Sacraments?

A. The Sacraments have a Primary Minister, and a Secondary Minister. The Primary Minister is

Jesus Christ, who is the Author of the Sacraments; the Secondary Minister is he who has received from Jesus Christ authority to confer them. Who are the different ministers of the different sacraments we shall see when we come to speak of each sacrament in particular. I merely remark here that the Council of Trent has defined, against heretics, that not *all* Christians are ministers of all the sacraments; to affirm the contrary, therefore, would be heresy.

Are faith and sanctifying grace requisite in the Minister of the Sacraments?

A. In order that he may confer them *worthily* and *with merit* it is undoubtedly requisite that he have faith, and that he be in a state of grace; but in respect of the *validity* of the sacrament it is an article of the Faith, that neither the one nor the other is requisite; and so Baptism, conferred by an impious heretic, has the same validity as if conferred by a pious catholic.

Is *intention* necessary in the Minister?

A. It is of Faith, that in conferring the Sacraments, it is necessary to have the intention of doing what the Church does; without such intention the Minister would confer the Sacrament invalidly.

Suppose heretics, who do not believe in the Holy Catholic Church, or idolaters, Turks, &c., who attach no value to the Sacraments, were to administer Baptism, would they not administer it invalidly, because they could have no intention of doing what the Church does : for in regard to heretics, they do not believe in her, and in regard to idolaters, Turks, and Jews, they believe neither in her nor in her sacraments ?

A. It is not necessary for the validity of the sacrament that the Minister intend to do a holy action, to confer a sacrament, nor that he believe in the virtue of the Sacraments, nor that he have the intention of doing what the true Catholic and Roman Church does ; it is sufficient that he have the intention of doing what the Church in general does. So a Lutheran, who supposes that the true Church exists in his sect, when he baptizes with the intention of doing what the Church does, baptizes validly. In like manner, if a Turk, to annoy and spite another Turk, should seriously baptize a child, intending to give him the Baptism of the Christians, that child would be validly baptized.

Would Baptism, Absolution, or any other sacrament be valid, if given in sport and jest ?

A. They would be invalid, as was declared by Holy Church against Luther. Hence if any one should take an unbaptized child, pour water on his head, and utter the form, saying : " This is what the Parish Priest will do when he baptizes him," that child would not be baptized. Observe that such jesting in regard to the Sacraments is mortal sin.

What sort of intention is required in him who is the Minister of the Sacraments ?

A. The intention may be *actual*, as, for example, when he who baptizes says to himself, whilst he baptizes: "I intend to baptize;" or it may be *virtual*, as, for example, when one sets out with the intention of baptizing, and afterwards in the act of baptizing, from some distraction does not reflect on what he is doing. Or, finally, the intention may be *habitual*, as, for example, when one who is accustomed to baptize, administers this sacrament, at a time that from some disease he is deprived of the use of reason. The first is not necessary; the second suffices; but not so the third, because with it the Minister of the Sacrament does not perform a human act.

What intention is required in those who receive the Sacraments?

A. It is most certain that no intention whatever is required to receive the Sacrament of Baptism in children before the use of reason, and in adults who have never had free use of reason. Moreover it is an express article of the Faith, that Baptism, conferred on children before the use of reason, is valid, as we gather from the Sacred Council of Trent, and from the practice of the universal Church of baptizing children as soon as they are born. But, on the other hand, in adults who have perfect use of reason, or, at least, who have once had it, it is necessary, either that they have actually the will to receive Baptism, or that, having had that will, they have not retracted it. Such will is still more requisite in the Sacraments of Penance, Matrimony, and perhaps even of Order.* To receive the Sacraments of Confirmation, the ·Eucharist and Extreme Unction, however, *interpretative* intention suffices : which consists in this, that he who wishes to be a Christian, wishes also to enjoy all the privileges and graces of a Christian, and therefore also the graces of these Sacraments.

You think then that a sick person, deprived of his senses, would receive Confirmation, the Eucharist and Extreme Unction with profit, although he might not, while in his senses, have asked for these Sacraments ?

A. If he were in the grace of God he would receive them with profit, or, at all events, if, before the loss of his senses, he had had a sincere sorrow of attrition, as we pointed out in the answer to the twelfth question. It is evident from the practice of the Church, which in early times gave the Eucharist to infants, that these Sacraments may be received with profit, without that positive intention which the other Sacraments require. It is even now permitted to give Confirmation to infants, in cases where there is good reason to fear that they will not be able to receive it when they shall have attained the use of reason, as we shall shew in §. iii. Extreme Unction is given to sick persons

---

* It has been matter of controversy among Theologians whether the Sacrament of Order can be *validly* administered to children.

deprived of their senses, not only when they have previously asked for it, but even when, from unforeseen attacks, they have not had time to ask for it, and are in immediate danger of death. This the Church would not have permitted, were it necessary to have a positive intention in order to receive these Sacraments with profit. Observe, however, that the Eucharist must not be given to sick persons wholly deprived of their senses, by reason of the irreverence which might occur in such cases.

Is it an article of the Faith that there are Seven Sacraments?

A. It is an article of the Faith, expressly defined by the Sacred Council of Trent; and so he would be a heretic who should assert that there are more than seven Sacraments, or less than seven Sacraments. They are :—Baptism, Confirmation, the Eucharist, Penance, Extreme Unction, Order, and Matrimony.

What is required in a sacred rite, in order that it may be called a Sacrament of the New Law?

(A. There must be an *external* sign, *Divine institution*, and power *of conferring* grace. These three things united are only found in the foresaid seven Sacraments, recognised in the Catholic Church.

SECT. II.   *Baptism.*

How do you define the Sacrament of Baptism?

A. It is a Sacrament of the New Law, instituted by Christ, for the spiritual regeneration of man.

What do these words, *for the spiritual regeneration of man*, signify?

A. Man, by sin, is born dead to the grace of God, and by means of Baptism, he is born again to this grace, which is the supernatural life of the soul. In this spiritual regeneration, he is admitted to make part of Christ's faithful, that is to say, he becomes a member of His Church, and he acquires the right to receive the other Sacraments.

What is the *matter* of this Sacrament?

A. Natural water, whether from a well, a spring, or from the sea. In *Solemn* Baptism, however, that is, in Baptism conferred with the accustomed ceremonies, the holy water, blessed in the Font on Holy Saturday, should be used.

Would not any other liquid, such as wine, oil, &c., suffice in case of necessity, for the administration of Baptism?

A. It is of faith that true, natural water is necessary for the valid administration of Baptism. Hence if any other liquid whatsoever were made use of, the Baptism would be invalid.

Suppose that true, natural water were used, but that some other liquid or matter were mixed with it, in that case would the Baptism be likewise invalid?

A. If a small quantity of other matter were mixed with the water, the Baptism would not be invalid: we see, in fact, that a little Oil and Chrism is mixed with the water which is blessed in the Font on Holy Saturday, and this is the water which, except in case of necessity, ought to be used for baptizing. If, however, the liquid or other matter mixed with the water were in such quantity that it could no longer be called water—if, for example, so much earth were mixed with the water that it became mud—in that case the Baptism would be invalid, that is to say, it would have no effect.

What is the form of the Sacrament of Baptism?

A. "I baptize thee in the Name of the Father, and of the Son, and of the Holy Ghost."

Would the Baptism be invalid if any one of these words were changed, or omitted to be expressed?

A. If the change or omission were not *essential*, the Baptism would be valid, but if essential, then it would be invalid. For instance, if the word *Ego* were omitted, the Baptism would retain its effect; but if the word *baptizo* were omitted, it would have no virtue whatever.

To what must attention be paid in the act of baptizing?

A. To pouring water over the head of the child, in such quantity that it flow over the head, pronouncing meanwhile, with great precision, the words of the form.

Why must attention be paid to pouring water *over the head?*

A. Because, although the Baptism might probably be valid if the water were poured over any other part of the body, especially if it were any principal part, such as the breast or shoulders, still its validity would not be so certain as if it were poured over the head. And therefore it is prescribed by the Roman Ritual, that, if a child shall have been baptized on any other part of the body, he is to be re-baptized under condition. Moreover, in pouring water upon the head, care must be taken that it does not merely flow upon the hair, if the person baptized have thick hair, because some doubt whether, unless the water touch the skin, the Baptism be valid. There is small foundation for this doubt, but as to a sacrament of so great necessity, we should adopt every precaution, and so take care that the water flow over the forehead or temples.

Why is it requisite that water should be poured in such quantity *as to flow ?*

A. Because Baptism is a washing, and it could not be called so unless the water flowed; we certainly could not say a thing was washed if only a few drops of water were let fall upon it, and remained where they fell.

Is it necessary that the water be poured three times over the head of the baptized ?

A. The Church so prescribes, and therefore this rite ought to be observed: the Baptism, however, would certainly be valid, even if the water were only poured once.

Why is it requisite that the form should be pronounced, at the same moment that the water is poured upon the head of the baptized?

A. Because, in all the Sacraments the form should always be applied to the matter, and if there were any considerable interval between pronouncing the form and applying the matter, the sacrament would be invalid.

Who is the Minister of the Sacrament of Baptism?

A. The *ordinary* Minister of the Sacrament of Baptism is a Priest, the *extraordinary* Minister of this sacrament is a Deacon, who, when there is just cause, may be delegated to administer it with the accustomed ceremonies. Should it happen, however, that neither Priest nor Deacon can be had, then any person, even a child, provided he have the use of reason, nay, even an infidel, may administer Baptism. This is defined by the fourth Lateran Council.

If a Cleric not yet ordained Deacon, or a layman should baptize a child when it was not a case of necessity, would such Baptism be valid?

A. It would be valid, certainly : but it would be a grave sin for any ordinary person to presume to baptize, when it was not a case of necessity.

Is Baptism necessary for every one?

A. Baptism is necessary for all, in order that they

may attain eternal salvation ; and this is an article
of the Faith defined by the Sacred Council of
Trent.   Theologians, however, distinguish three
sorts of Baptism : the Baptism of Blood, the Baptism of Desire, and the Baptism of Water.   This
latter alone is properly a Sacrament ; the other two
may stand in place of the Sacrament, but they are
not Sacraments.⟩

What is the Baptism of Blood?

A. The Baptism of Blood is Martyrdom.   If a
child were killed out of hatred to the Faith, before
he had been baptized, he would be saved.   When,
during the persecutions, adult Christians, and even
their infants were killed, such infants, although not
baptized, were saved.

What is the Baptism of Desire?

A. The desire to receive Baptism.   If a Turk,
finding himself at the point of death, desired Baptism, but had no one at hand to baptize him, he
would be saved.

What is requisite to constitute Martyrdom?

A. In the case of children, it is required that they
be killed out of hatred to Christ and His Faith ;
nothing more is requisite.   In this way the Holy
Innocents whom Herod caused to be put to death,
were truly martyrs.   In the case of adults, however, it is required: 1. That they accept death from
a right and supernatural motive, hence should any
one accept martyrdom out of vain-glory, in order
to be honoured as a martyr, his death would not

have the merit of martyrdom ; nor, should any one accept it, in order to free himself from a life made grievous to him by indigence, would he be a martyr. 2. That they have no will to defend themselves ; because to die in battle for the Faith is not properly martyrdom. 3. In the case of one guilty of mortal sin, repentance of his sin, at least by attrition, is requisite. Observe also, that martyrdom, being an act of the virtue of fortitude, should be *voluntary.* It is not, however, necessary to have the actual will, nor even the virtual will of meeting death in order to bear witness to the Faith ; the *habitual* will suffices. For example, in time of persecution, a Christian, resolved to die rather than to renounce his Faith, were he surprised by the persecutors whilst asleep, and killed, would be a true martyr because of such habitual disposition. Observe, further, that martyrdom does not free a man from all his other obligations at the point of death, if he has time to fulfil them. If he has not been baptized, he is obliged, if possible, to receive Baptism ; and in the case of a baptized person, if he have any mortal sin on his soul still unconfessed, he would be obliged to confess it, were there a Priest at hand to absolve him.

Would one be a martyr who should suffer death, in order not to offend against some other virtue, as, for example, against chastity ?

A. Certainly ; and the virgins who suffered death, rather than yield to the seductions of those who attempted their chastity, are venerated as martyrs.

Can those be called true martyrs, who suffer death through their charity in serving the sick in time of pestilence?

A. They could not be called martyrs, in the strict sense of the term, because martyrdom is an act of the virtue of Fortitude in defence of the Faith, or of some other Christian virtue; and in exposing themselves to danger of death by serving the plague-stricken, they make an act of Fortitude, not in *defence* of the virtue of charity, but in the *practice* of it. Still, in God's sight, this may have a merit equal to that of real martyrdom; and the Church in her Martyrology of the 28th of February, venerates as martyrs those who died in the service of the sick in time of pestilence.*

Does martyrdom supply all the effects of Baptism?

A. Martyrdom supplies by infusion of grace and remission of sins, but it cannot supply the other effects of Baptism, of which we shall speak presently; and for which the Baptism of Water, that is, the sacrament, is requisite. With regard to the remission of sins, you must observe that in martyrdom they are all remitted with the same fulness with which they are remitted in Baptism, so that the martyr has no remains of temporal punish-

---

* Quos velut martyres religiosa fides venerare consuevit. "Them a religious faith is wont to venerate as martyrs."

ment to suffer in the other life, but no sooner is his martyrdom consummated, than he is admitted to the estate of eternal beatitude.

In case of necessity, is the simple desire of Baptism sufficient for the attainment of eternal salvation?

A. The simple desire of Baptism is not sufficient if it be not accompanied by an act of contrition, or of charity; because, apart from the Sacrament, save in the case of martyrdom, sins are not remitted without contrition, that is to say, unless the sinner detests them from the motive of the pure love of God.

Is it, however, certain that children can be validly baptized?

A: It is an article of the Faith, defined by the Sacred Council of Trent, and he who should say that children so baptized are not really Christians, or that, on attaining the use of reason, they ought to be re-baptized, or that it is better to defer Baptism till they have attained the use of reason, would be a heretic, and excommunicated by the said Council.

Supposing children, on attaining the use of reason, are dissatisfied at having been baptized, are they in such case bound to live as Christians?

A. Baptism constitutes them subjects of Holy Church; hence they would be bound to live as Christians; nor must any attention be paid to their dissatisfaction, it being most unreasonable and unjust.

But would not this be to do violence to conscience ?

' A. To oblige a person to do what is his positive duty, cannot be called doing violence to conscience. If men, who are constituted subjects of the Church through Baptism, could, when they attain the use of reason, refuse to remain subjects to the Church ; much more could they, when they attain the use of reason, refuse to submit to the authority of the lawful government of the state in which they are born. I say *much more*, because the authority which the Church has over baptized persons is more sacred and inviolable, than the authority which any sovereign has over his people. In fact, we are not made subjects by any sacrament, nor do we receive any indelible character constituting us such in perpetuity in regard to the lawful sovereign in whose states we are born. If we change our country we are no longer his subjects. But we can go to no part of the world where we can withdraw ourselves from subjection to the Church, after having been once baptized.*

What are the effects of Baptism ?

A. There are six effects of the Sacrament of

---

* By this we do not mean to say that the authority which the sovereign has over his subjects is not sacred and inviolable. It is sacred because princes derive their authority from God ; and inviolable because, except in case of a prince commanding what would be a crime, and which case would be not a use of authority but an abuse of power, it cannot happen that subjects should have the right to disobey their sovereign.

Baptism. 1. It remits original sin and every actual sin, as well in respect of the guilt, as in respect of even the temporal punishment due to actual sin ; so that, should an adult pass out of this life immediately after having received Baptism, he would have no debt of temporal punishment to pay in Purgatory ; and therefore, if an adult were baptized when dying, no indulgence could be given him. 2. It confers sanctifying grace, infused virtues, and the other supernatural gifts whereby a man is sanctified and interiorly renewed. 3. It gives a certain right of receiving the actual graces necessary to attainment of his end, that is to say, the graces necessary to enable a man to live a Christian and holy life. This last constitutes the *sacramental grace* of which we have spoken in the preceding Sect., A. 15. 4. It imprints an indelible character on the soul ; and for this reason, Baptism can be received but once. 5. It constitutes us members of the Church ; and subjects us to her jurisdiction. 6. It gives us the capability, and the right to receive the other Sacraments ; and it makes us participators in the common treasures of the Church, such as indulgences, the fruits of the Sacrifice of the Mass, &c.

When adults receive Baptism, ought they to have sorrow for their sins ?

A. They need not have sorrow for original sin, because we can only repent of sins which we have committed from our own proper, individual, personal malice. It is certain, however, that they ought to repent of actual mortal sins, at least with the sorrow of attrition, because those sins are forgiven to no one who has not sorrow for them.

Sect. III.   *Confirmation.*

How do you define the Sacrament of Confirmation?

A. Confirmation is a Sacrament of the New Law, by which the strength of the Holy Spirit is given to baptized persons, in order that they may remain firm in the Faith, and profess it intrepidly.

Who is the Minister of this Sacrament?

A. It is an article of the Faith, declared by the Sacred Council of Trent, that Bishops alone are the *ordinary* Ministers of this Sacrament. The Supreme Pontiff can, however, delegate even a simple Priest to confer Confirmation. In such case, that Priest is the *extraordinary* Minister of this Sacrament.

What is the Matter in Confirmation?

A. The imposition of hands, and the unction of the Sacred Chrism.

What is the Form in Confirmation?

A. These words : "I sign thee with the sign of the Cross. I confirm thee with the Chrism of Salvation."

Who are the subjects of this Sacrament?

A. All baptized persons ; hence it was in ancient times given to infants immediately after Baptism ; although now, according to the present discipline of the Church, it ought not to be conferred on children under seven years of age, except in cases of necessity.

What dispositions are requisite in those who receive this Sacrament?

A. When the Bishop believes there is sufficient cause to confer this Sacrament on children before the use of reason, all that is required is, that they should have been baptized. But when this Sacrament is conferred on adults, or on children who have attained the use of reason, it is required that they be in a state of grace, and that they be properly instructed in matters of Faith, and in regard to the nature and effects of this Sacrament.

Is this Sacrament necessary in order to the attainment of eternal salvation?

A. It is not *necessary* absolutely speaking; for otherwise simple Priests would have been the Ministers of this Sacrament, in order that it might be an easy matter for all to receive it. Still, every one who has it in his power, is obliged to receive this Sacrament under pain of mortal sin; as Benedict XIV. commanded the Bishops to teach those who had not yet received it.

What are the effects of this Sacrament?

A. There are two: 1. The indelible character; as we have shewn in the 1st Sect. A. 17. 2. The fulness of the Holy Spirit, which gives a special strength to the soul, enabling it easily to overcome temptations against the Faith, and to endure with invincible constancy persecutions for its sake. This fulness of the Holy Spirit includes also increase of sanctifying grace.

SECT. IV. *The Holy Eucharist.*

Is the Holy Eucharist a Sacrament of the New Law?

A. It is a true Sacrament of the New Law, and that it is so is an express article of the Faith.

Is it also a true Sacrifice?

A. It is likewise an express article of the Faith, that the Holy Eucharist is a true Sacrifice.

How do you define the Holy Eucharist,—as it is a Sacrament?

A. The Holy Eucharist is a Sacrament of the New Law, which really contains the Body and Blood of Jesus Christ under the species of bread and wine, and was instituted for the spiritual refection of the Faithful.

What is the *Matter* of this Sacrament?

A. Bread made of wheat, and wine made of grapes.

What is the *Form* of this Sacrament?

A. The words of consecration which the Priest pronounces over the bread and wine in the Holy Mass.

What change is wrought in the bread and wine when the words of consecration are pronounced?

A. It is an article of the Faith that the whole

substance of the bread is changed into the Body of Jesus Christ, and that the whole substance of the wine is changed into His Blood.

Why do you say *the whole substance?*

A. Because it is an article of the Faith, declared by the Church against certain heretics, that, after the words of Consecration, there remains nothing of the substance of the bread and of the wine, but that it is all changed into the Body and Blood of Christ; and to denote that the *species,* that is, the colour, smell, taste, and quantity, as well of the bread as of the wine, remain ; and so, these substances being changed into the Body and Blood of Christ, there remain the appearances of bread and wine.

Then, in the consecrated Host there is only the Body, and in the consecrated chalice there is only the Blood of Christ ?

A. This would be a heresy, for it is of Faith that Whole Christ, and therefore His Soul and His Divinity, is as well in the Host under the species of bread, as in the chalice under the species of wine. We say that the bread is changed into the Body of Christ, and the wine into His Blood, because by virtue of the words of Consecration the bread is changed into His Body, which, as a living body, contains His Blood ; and because, by virtue of the words of Consecration of the chalice, the wine is changed into the Blood of Christ, which, as living blood, is united to His Body, and so *by concomi-*

tance His Blood is along with His Body, and His Body along with His Blood.

Then we receive the Living and Whole Christ as much under the species of bread, as under the species of wine ?

A. Certainly ; and this is an article of the Faith.

What kind of bread ought to be consecrated ?

A. Any kind of bread, provided it be made of wheaten flour, can be validly consecrated ; and so, whether the bread be made with leaven or without leaven, by the words of Consecration it is changed into the Body of the Lord. You must observe, however, that the Church commands us to use bread made without leaven, and prohibits the consecration of leavened bread. At the same time, many of the Greeks having an ancient custom of consecrating leavened bread, the Church permits this use *to them ;* nay, not only permits it, but desires that it be maintained.

Would it not be well that lay persons also, when they communicate, should receive the Blessed Sacrament under the species of wine, as well as under the species of bread ?

A. For many wise reasons the Church has pro- hibited the administration of the Blessed Sacrament to lay persons under the species of wine ; nor can even priests communicate under the species of wine, except when they celebrate the Holy Mass. More- over, it would be a heresy, condemned by the Sacred Council of Trent, to say that Christians are obliged to communicate also under the species of wine. Observe further, that, receiving the Living and Whole Christ, as well under the species of bread as under the species of wine, he who receives Him only under the species of bread, is not defrauded of any part of the fruit of the Sacrament.

When a consecrated host is divided, what happens to the Body of Christ ?

A. No change nor alteration takes place in the Body of Christ; but it is of Faith that when the Host is broken into small particles—the Living and Whole Christ is under each particle—and the same happens if the species of wine in the chalice is divided into small drops.

For how long a time does the Body and the Blood of Christ remain really present in the Blessed Sacrament ?

A. It is an article of the Faith, that the Body and Blood of Christ remain present therein so long as the species are not consumed, or have become corrupted. Therefore, if the species of wine were left in the chalice until it evaporated, or became vinegar, there would no longer be the Blood of Christ in that chalice.

When we communicate, for how long a time does the Real Presence of Christ remain in us ?

A. It remains in us so long as the heat of the stomach does not change the sacramental species; therefore, according to the greater or less activity of the stomach, Christ remains a greater or less time really present in us.

Who is the Minister of the Sacrament of the Eucharist?

A. Priests alone can consecrate the bread and wine; therefore, not even in case of necessity can one who is not a Priest consecrate validly. Hence, for example, should a Deacon say Mass, he would not consecrate, and the bread would still remain bread, and the wine would still remain wine. This is of the Faith. Moreover, the *administration* of this Sacrament belongs also to Priests alone, so that no other, ordinarily speaking, can give communion. I say ordinarily speaking, because, in case of necessity, a Deacon also can give communion, and so Deacons are the *extraordinary* ministers of this Sacrament, not in respect of consecration, but of administration.

Who are the *subjects* of this Sacrament?

(A. All baptized persons are the subjects of this Sacrament, that is to say, they are capable of receiving it; but in adults, to receive it with profit, the necessary dispositions are requisite.)

May children then also receive Communion?

A. For many centuries it was the custom of the Church to give Communion to children before the use of reason, but this custom has now ceased; so that according to the present discipline of the Church, it is not lawful to give them Communion. Observe, moreover, that the Sacred Council of

Trent excommunicates those who should assert that Communion is necessary for children before they attain the use of reason.

What *dispositions* are requisite in adults?

A. Sanctifying grace; knowledge of the Sacrament, that is to say, that they know what they are receiving; and, except in the case of danger of death, fasting from every kind of food and drink, even though it were medicinal. These are the most essential dispositions; there are others which cause us to receive this Sacrament with greater fruits, but the masters of the spiritual life will instruct you in regard to these.

Suppose a person in mortal sin were about to communicate, would it suffice that he put himself in a state of grace by an act of perfect contrition?

A. In the 14th A. of the present chapter, Sect. I. we have said that it would not suffice, there being the precept of St. Paul, which obliges all those who would communicate, to go first to Confession every time they have been guilty of any mortal sin. This is meant speaking generally, for if there were urgent necessity to communicate, and no Confessor could be had, a person might receive Holy Communion with an act of perfect contrition alone. But it is for moralists to discuss such cases of necessity, as well as the obligation which remains of confessing the sin.

What are the *effects* of this Sacrament?

A. The first effect is spiritual nourishment of the

soul, through the increase of sanctifying grace ; the second effect is deliverance from venial sins ; the third, preservation from mortal sins. The Sacred Council of Trent assigns these effects to this Sacrament. The Councils of Florence and Vienne add a fourth effect, which is spiritual delectation ; this, however, as St. Bernard observes, is only conferred on those who are thoroughly detached from earthly affections, and very fervent in spirit. Such as these, when they communicate, experience in a sensible manner how sweet is the Lord.

What necessity is there to receive Holy Communion ?

A. All adults, by Divine and Ecclesiastical precept, are bound to communicate, and the Church has fixed this obligation at once a year, so that he who should not fulfil this obligation would not be saved. There is also obligation to communicate when death is approaching ; but moral theologians will tell you of these obligations. Observe, however, that this necessity is only *of precept*, so that should an adult find it impossible to receive Holy Communion, he might notwithstanding be saved.

Is the practice of daily Communion to be approved in the case of lay persons ?

A. It is doubtless to be approved. 1. Because such was the common practice of the early Church. 2. Because it is in comformity with the desire of the Council of Trent. 3. Because the Roman Catechism directs Parish Priests frequently to exhort the Faithful to practise it. 4. Because a decree of the Sacred Congregation, approved by Innocent XI., forbids that even married persons, or those engaged in business, should be debarred from daily Communion, and orders it to be left to the judgment of Confessors as to who shall be admitted, or not admitted to it. Much more is daily Communion to be approved for persons living in religious communities.

You said that the Blessed Eucharist is not only a Sacrament, but that it is also a true Sacrifice. I should like, in the first place, to know what a Sacrifice is ?

A. A Sacrifice may be defined as—an oblation or offering of a sensible thing, made to God by His legitimate Minister, in recognition of His supreme dominion over all creatures,—and this offering must import some destruction of the thing or victim which is offered : otherwise, should this destruction be wanting, it is no longer a Sacrifice, but a simple Oblation. This definition belongs also to the Sacrifices of the Old Law, in which animals were offered to God by lawful Priests, in recognition of His supreme authority, and they offered them by putting them to death.

How can this definition be applied to the Holy Eucharist ?

A. In the Holy Mass there is the oblation of a sensible thing, that is, of the Body and Blood of Jesus Christ, under the species of bread and wine.

There is a legitimate minister, that is, the Priest, and there is the immolation or destruction of a victim, which immolation was made *really* in the Sacrifice of the Cross, when Jesus Christ really shed His Blood, and really died ; but in the Holy Mass this immolation is made *mystically*, for Jesus Christ does not shed His Blood any more, nor die any more really, but mystically, inasmuch as *by virtue of the words* of Consecration the Body alone of Christ is made present under the species of bread, and the Blood alone of Christ under the species of wine ; and although along with His Body there is also His Blood, and along with His Blood there is also His Body, this happens not by virtue of the words of Consecration, but by way of *concomitance*, inasmuch as the Blood of Christ cannot now be again really separated from His Body. Therefore in the Mass, the Body and Blood of the Lord are offered *as if separated* under the diverse species of bread and wine ; and this suffices for mystical destruction or immolation of the victim.

What kind of sacrifice must we say is the Sacrifice of the Mass ?

A. The Sacred Council of Trent has defined that the Holy Mass is the same Sacrifice as that of the Cross, differing from it only as to the *manner* in which it is offered ; for the same Victim Who was offered then, is offered now upon our altars, that is to say, Jesus Christ, who was made a Victim for our sins, and it is the same Priest who offers that Victim, inasmuch as Jesus Christ is the principal offerer, offering Himself as He did upon Calvary, but through the ministry of His Priests. Therefore, (when Holy Mass is celebrated, the Sacrifice of the Cross is renewed ; which then was a Bloody Sacrifice, that is, with a real blood-shedding ; and now is an Unbloody Sacrifice, that is, with a not real but mystical blood-shedding.

(What are the qualities of the Sacrifice of the Holy Mass ?

A. It is *Latreutic,* that is to say, it is a Sacrifice of Praise, rendering infinite praise to God. It is *Eucharistic,* that is to say, it is a Sacrifice of Thanksgiving, which avails to thank Him for all possible benefits. It is *Propitiatory,* that is to say, it is such as to appease Him for all sins. It is *Impetratory,* that is to say, it can impetrate for us every grace.)

Had not the Sacrifice of the Cross all these characteristics, and was it not all-sufficient ? Why, then, must we acknowledge the Holy Mass to be a true Sacrifice ?

A. In the first place, you must observe, as St. Thomas shews, that the true Religion must have a Sacrifice to offer to God. Now we have no other Sacrifice, for the ancient sacrifices were abrogated ; and therefore, if it were not for the Holy Mass, the Christian religion could offer no Sacrifice to God. In the second place, observe that, although the Sacrifice of the Cross was all-sufficient, and more than all-sufficient, yet by the Holy Mass the honour which God received from the Sacrifice of the Cross is renewed; and it is a most powerful means, by which the merits of that same Sacrifice, which our Saviour offered upon the Cross, are applied to us.

Does the Sacrifice of the Holy Mass aid only the living?

A. It is an article of the Faith, defined by the Sacred Council of Trent, that the Sacrifice of the Holy Mass aids not only the living, but also the dead who are in Purgatory.

Can Masses be celebrated in honour of the Saints?

A. It is likewise an article of the Faith, defined in the said Council, that it is well to celebrate Masses in honour of the Saints. Observe, however, that the Holy Sacrifice can only be offered to God in thanksgiving for the great graces which he has bestowed upon the Saints, and to obtain their patronage. Hence the Holy Mass can be offered to no Saint, but only to God, in thanksgiving for the graces which He has bestowed upon them, and in order that He may deign to make us partakers of their intercession. Nevertheless, since all this redounds to the honour of the Saints, we say rightly that Masses are celebrated in honour of the Saints.

Who can offer the Sacrifice of the Holy Mass?

A. Jesus Christ, who instituted it at the Last Supper, and Who then thus offered a true Sacrifice of His Body and Blood under the species of bread and wine, is truly and properly the Principal Offerer of the Holy Mass. In the second place, Priests alone can, immediately and properly, as ministers, offer this Sacrifice, as we have already said ; nor could it be validly celebrated by any person what-ever who was not a Priest. In the third place, all the Faithful, as members of the Church, when they hear Holy Mass, offer the Holy Sacrifice together with the Priest, as appears from the prayers of the Canon.

If all the Faithful offer the Sacrifice together with the Priest, ought they not all to communicate when they hear Mass ?

A. It is well that all who are disposed should communicate. The Council of Trent desires that all who are present should dispose themselves to receive Holy Communion from the Priest who celebrates, as we have already shewn ; nevertheless, this is not a matter of necessity. Moreover, the same Council excommunicates any one who should assert that Holy Mass cannot be celebrated unless the assistants communicate.

Is it necessary to put a little water in the wine which is consecrated in Holy Mass ?

A. It is not necessary for *validity*, because, by the words of Consecration, the wine would be changed into the Blood of Christ, although no water were put into the chalice ; but it is necessary to add the water, because, as, as the Holy Fathers declare, Christ did so at the Last Supper, it has always been the custom of the Church, and the Church has most rigorously commanded it. Moreover, the Council of Trent excommunicates any one who should assert that this small quantity of water is not to be put in the wine. You must be careful, however, not to put too great a quantity of water into the chalice, because if the wine were mixed with much water, it would no longer be fit matter for the Consecration.

Would it not be better if the Holy Mass were celebrated in the vulgar tongue, and in a loud voice, so that the people might understand all the prayers?

A. He who should say that the Mass ought to be celebrated only in the vulgar tongue, and the whole of it, including the Canon and the words of Consecration, in a loud voice, would incur the excommunication fulminated by the Council of Trent. In like manner, he who should despise the ceremonies, rites, or vestments which are used in celebrating the Holy Mass, would incur the excommunication fulminated by the same Council.

SECT. V.—*Penance.*

Is Penance a Sacrament of the New Law?

A. Penance is a supernatural moral virtue, which inclines the sinner to detest and grieve for his sins, inasmuch as they are offences against God, and to have a purpose of amendment and satisfaction. This virtue was always necessary for sinners, even under

the old law, in order that they might obtain the
pardon of their sins, and Jesus Christ raised it to
the rank of a Sacrament, so that, when Penance has
the due requisites, according to the institution of
Christ, it is a true Sacrament.

Is not Penance then always a Sacrament?

A. When there is not only sorrow for sin committed, not only purpose of amendment, and of
making satisfaction to the Divine Justice,—but also
confession of sins made to a Priest approved for
confession, and absolution received from him, then
it is of faith that Penance is a true sacrament;
but when these two last are wanting, it is a simple
virtue.

How do you define the Sacrament of Penance?

A. Penance is a Sacrament, instituted by Jesus
Christ, in which, by the acts of the penitent and
the absolution of an approved priest, sins committed after Baptism are remitted.

What is the Matter of this Sacrament?

A. Sins committed after Baptism are the *remote*
matter of this Sacrament; Contrition, Confession
of the same sins, and Satisfaction are the *proximate*
matter.

Are all sins committed after Baptism equally
the matter of this Sacrament.

A. Mortal sins never previously confessed are
the *necessary* matter, so that, except in case of real
nability, they must be confessed in order to obtain

14

pardon ; venial sins, however, and all mortal sins
already confessed are *sufficient* matter ; so that there
is no *obligation* to confess them, but they *may* be
confessed, and, there being no other sins to confess, Absolution may be received for them.

Iu case of real inability, how are mortal sins forgiven without Confession ?

A. They are pardoned by means of perfect Contrition, which includes the desire or purpose of Confession, as we pointed out in Ch. 6, § iii.

Is it a good thing to frequent Confession, when
we have no mortal sins to confess ?

A. It is certainly a good thing, and conformable
to the desire of the Church, and the practice of
fervent Christians.

(What is Contrition ?)

A. The Council of Trent defines Contrition as
" a hearty sorrow and detestation of sins committed, accompanied by a purpose not to sin any
more."   Contrition is perfect when this sorrow
springs from perfect love of God.   It is imperfect
when it springs from a supernatural motive, indeed,
but not from the perfect love of God.   If a person
repents of having offended God because he has
offended the Supreme Good who merits to be
loved above everything, he has perfect contrition.
If, on the other hand, he repents for having forfeited
Heaven and merited Hell, he has imperfect contrition.

Is perfect or imperfect Contrition necessary for Confession?

' A. Perfect Contrition is undoubtedly desirable, but it is not necessary; since otherwise every one who went to Confession would go already in a state of grace, there being no doubt, as we have said in Ch. 6, § iii. that perfect Charity and perfect Contrition place the soul in the grace of God, before receiving Sacramental Absolution, and that, too, apart from case of necessity. Imperfect Contrition therefore suffices for Confession.

What conditions ought Contrition, that is, sorrow for sin, to have?

A. It must be *internal,* that is to say, it must come from the heart : it must be *supreme,* that is to say, it must cause us to detest sin above every other evil ; it must be *universal,* making us abhor all mortal sins whatsoever ; it must be *supernatural,* that is to say, it must spring from a motive revealed by the Holy Faith.

Is a sorrow which has these conditions necessary in Confession, when we have only to accuse ourselves of venial sins?

A. There is no doubt of it, except in regard to the third condition ; for it is not necessary that the penitent should have an universal sorrow for all his venial sins ; it is sufficient that, when confessing only venial sins, he should repent of some one of them. He must, however, have an internal, supreme, supernatural sorrow on account of that of which he repents, so that he may be disposed to suffer anything whatever, rather than commit it any more.

Could a person who had only venial sins to confess, and who did not feel this sorrow, go to Confession ?

A. Such an one could not receive Absolution, otherwise the Sacrament would be void, as wanting an essential part.   On this account Theologians advise persons who frequent Holy Confession and who accuse themselves only of habitual venial sins, to add to their confession some graver sin of their past life for which they have a more certain sorrow, in order that the matter of the Sacrament may not be wanting.   For want of such caution it is possible that not a few persons who frequent Holy Confession receive Absolution in vain.   But we leave this to be discussed by Moral Theologians.

Of what sort ought our purpose of amendment to be ?

A. Our purpose of amendment must be *firm,* that is to say, the will must be resolute never more to return to the sin which we detest; it must be *universal,* so that it be resolute to guard against committing any mortal sin whatsoever: it must be *efficacious,* so that it be disposed to adopt all the necessary means to avoid sin.

What is Confession?

A. Confession is accusation of one's own sins, committed after Baptism, made by the penitent, in the presence of the Priest, in order to obtain Absolution.

Can we not obtain pardon of mortal sins without confessing them?

A. This is an article of the Faith, defined by the Sacred Council of Trent, because there is an express Divine Command to confess all and each of our mortal sins; and if the pardon of such mortal sins is obtained by means of perfect contrition, it is obtained because in that perfect contrition there is included the purpose or desire of confession.

How often are we under obligation to fulfil this precept?

A. Generally speaking, there is obligation to fulfil it once a year, and at the point of death. There may, however, be other circumstances which also oblige us to fulfil this precept, as may be seen in the Moral Theology.

What is Satisfaction?

A. Satisfaction, which is a part of the Sacrament of Penance, is the acceptance, and voluntary fulfilment of the Penance enjoined by the confessor, in order to compensate for the injury we have done to God by the sin.

The guilt of sin being pardoned, do we remain debtors to any punishment?

A. Contrition is sometimes so powerful and vehement that it takes away not only the guilt, but also all the punishment : but for the most part, as the Council of Trent teaches, there remains a debt of temporal punishment due for sin, after the guilt is pardoned, and we must satisfy this either by works of penance in this life, or in Purgatory in the next.

It seems to me that the penance should be performed before receiving Absolution ?

A. The practice of the Church is contrary to this, which enjoins a penance and, if he who confesses his sins be rightly disposed, gives Absolution immediately, leaving him to perform the penance enjoined afterwards. Moreover, the Church has condemned certain modern rigorists, who pretended that the penance enjoined by the confessor ought to be performed before receiving Absolution.

Is the penance enjoined by the Confessor an essential part of the Sacrament ?

A. It is not an *essential* part of the Sacrament, for, in cases where it cannot be imposed or cannot be fulfilled, the Sacrament still produces its effect, that is, the justification of the sinner. On the other hand, it is a *necessary* part of the Sacrament, for it is of Divine precept that this penance should be imposed and performed, except in cases where there is an impossibility of fulfilling it. Therefore, should any one go to confession with the intention of not performing his penance, he would have a bad intention, which would render him ill disposed, and he would receive the Absolution unworthily, and his sins would not be forgiven him.

Is this penance entirely in the power of the Confessor ?

A. It is not in such manner in the power of the Confessor, that he can impose penances according to his own caprice ; but it is so far in the power of the Confessor, that, after prudently considering the number and quality of the sins, and the dispositions of the penitent, it rests with him to assign such penance as he shall prudently judge to be most fitting and salutary ; such penance being directed, as the Sacred Council of Trent teaches, not only as a punishment for past sins, but also as a remedy to preserve from future sins.

What is the Form of the Sacrament of Penance ?

A. " I absolve thee from thy sins, in the Name of the Father, and of the Son, and of the Holy Ghost." These last words, however, are not essential, for though he who should omit them would sin by so doing, the Absolution would be valid. The essential words are : " I absolve thee."

What is the meaning of these words ?

A. The meaning of these words is : "I administer to thee the Sacrament of Absolution." This is the explanation of St. Thomas. Or: "I give thee, in so far as I can, the grace which reconciles, or which remits sins." In this sense the form is true, even for those who approach the Sacrament already freed from sin, by perfect contrition, and who in reality could not have their sins taken away, because they have been taken away already. In such sense the form is true; because the sinner receives grace which, of its nature, is directed to the taking away of sin; because he reconciles himself more perfectly to God, and advances in His friendship; and because in the sacrament a part of the temporal pain due to sin is condoned.

Who is the Minister of the Sacrament of Penance?

A. Only Priests who have been approved for the hearing of confessions. All Priests who have cure of souls, are so approved, and also all others on whom jurisdiction to hear confessions has been conferred.

Who can give Priests jurisdiction to hear Confessions?

A. The Pope for the whole Church, as Universal Pastor; a Bishop in his own diocese; and a Regular Prelate to the religious subject to him. Observe, however, that Regulars cannot hear the confessions of Nuns, even of those who are exempt from the jurisdiction of the Bishop and subject to the Regular Prelate, without the approbation of the Bishop of the place.

Cannot priests, not approved for the hearing of confessions, absolve from venial sins?

A. It is certain that they cannot absolve even from venial sins, as was declared by the Congregation of Cardinals under Innocent XI., in 1679.

Can some sins be reserved, so that priests otherwise approved for the hearing of confessions, shall not have jurisdiction in regard of such sins?

A. It is an article of the Faith, declared in the Sacred Council of Trent, that Bishops can reserve to themselves certain sins, for which ordinary confessors cannot give absolution; and what each Bishop can do for his own Diocese, the Pope can do for the whole Church.

The Church orders that all the Faithful shall confess once a year to their own priest; what is meant by *their own* priest?

A. By their own priest is meant the Parish Priest; at the present day, however, it is sufficient to confess to any priest approved by the Bishop; such is the present practice recognized by the Supreme Pontiff, and by all the Bishops.

What are the effects of the Sacrament of Penance?

A. Five principal effects may be enumerated: 1, the remission of sin, and of the eternal punishment which sin merits, if it be mortal; 2, the diminution of the temporal punishment due to sin, a diminution greater or less, according to the more or less perfect disposition of the penitent; 3, renewal of friendship with God, which has been violated; 4, the restitution or revival of virtues and merits which have been lost by sin; 5, the aids of actual grace, that is to say, a certain right to have such aids in time of need, by means of which the penitent is strengthened against falling anew into sin, and strengthened to persevere in good.

What is meant by the virtues or *merits being restored* which have been lost by sin?

A. Sin causes us to lose the habits of virtue; the sin of infidelity, for example, causes us to lose Faith; the sin of despair causes us to lose Hope, &c.; and by means of a good confession these virtues are restored to the soul. Similarly, sin strips the soul of all the merits it had acquired for Eternal Life, and by means of confession those merits are restored to the soul.

APPENDIX. *On Indulgences.*

WHAT is an Indulgence ?

A. An Indulgence is a remission of the temporal punishment, which remains due to us, on account of our sins, after their guilt has been pardoned; which remission is given us outside the sacrament, by those who have the faculty to dispense the spiritual treasures of the Church.

Explain this to me more distinctly.

A. An Indulgence is said to be a remission of *punishment*, because it is not the *sin* which is remitted by the Indulgence, but the punishment due for the sin. It is said to be a remission of *temporal* punishment, because the eternal punishment due to mortal sin is not remitted by the Indulgence : that is remitted only in the Sacrament of Penance. This temporal punishment remains due after the guilt is pardoned, because, as we have already shewn, after Absolution has been received, there remains, for the most part, some debt of temporal punishment, which we must satisfy, either by works of penance in this life, or by Purgatory in the next. Observe further : this remission is given *outside the Sacrament*, which means that we must not confound an Indulgence with the remission of that part of the temporal punishment which is obtained by virtue of the Sacrament of Penance, in proportion to the more or less perfect dispositions of the penitent. In conclusion, the Indulgence is given by those who have the faculty to dispense, &c., because no one can grant Indulgences who has not legitimate authority to distribute the common treasures of the Church. The Pope has this power, without limit, for the whole Church ; the Bishops have it, limited, for their own Dioceses, and restricted by the Fourth Lateran Council, so that they can only grant Indulgences of forty days, and of one year in the Dedication of a Basilica.

Of what does the spiritual treasury of the Church consist ?

A. The spiritual treasury of the Church is formed of the infinite merits of Jesus Christ and of the Blessed Virgin Mary and of all the Saints; also of the merits of the just still living upon earth, as Clement VI. teaches in his Bull Unigenitus of the year 1350. The Church has authority to dispense these treasures, in remission of the temporal punishment due to God on account of sin.

Is it certain that in the Church there is this power to grant Indulgences ?

A. It is an article of the Faith, as declared by the Sacred Council of Trent.

Are there different kinds of Indulgences ?

A. Some Indulgences are *plenary*, and some *partial*. Plenary Indulgences remit the whole of the temporal punishment due to the Divine Justice. Hence, to obtain the full effect of a Plenary Indulgence, it is necessary not only to be in a state of grace, but also to be detached from all affection to venial sin. Partial Indulgences remit a part of the temporal punishment corresponding to forty days, seven years, or the like, of the penances formerly imposed.

What was this penance *formerly* imposed?

A. In early times, for many sins the Canons appointed penances either of days or years, which penances were to be performed by sinners when they were converted to God; these penances were called *the pains* imposed. They are now no longer prescribed; but when an Indulgence of forty days, seven years, or the like, is granted, so much temporal punishment is remitted, as would have been remitted to the penitent, had he fulfilled a penance of forty days, seven years, &c.

Can Indulgences be given also for the dead?

A. They can, and such is the practice of the Church. You must observe, however, that to the living, over whom the Church has jurisdiction, they are given by way of *absolution;* to the dead, over whom the Church has no longer jurisdiction, they are given by way of *suffrage.*

Sect. VI. *Extreme Unction.*

Is Extreme Unction a Sacrament?

A. That it is a true Sacrament is an article of the Faith, as defined by the Council of Trent.

What is the *Matter* of this Sacrament?

A. The Matter of this Sacrament is the Oil blessed by the Bishop on Maunday Thursday.

What is the *Form ?*.

A. The Prayer which is offered by the Priest, while he is anointing the senses of the sick person.

Who is the *Minister* of it ?

A. Priests alone are Ministers of this Sacrament.

Who are the *Subjects* of it ?

A. Sick persons alone, in peril of 'death, who have arrived at the use of reason; because for children who have not yet sinned such a form could not be used as : " By this holy anointing, and by His most piteous mercy, the Lord pardon thee, whereinsoever thou hast sinned by seeing, hearing, &c."

What are the *Effects* of this Sacrament ?

A. The first is *sanctifying grace*, with a right to actual graces given to comfort and strengthen the soul of the sick person amidst the pains and troubles of his sickness, and against the temptations of the devil. The second is to free him from the *relics of sin*, which are the weakness, languor, tepidity in good, anxiety and timidity which sin leaves behind it in the soul ; besides this, the temporal punishments still due to sin (see Sec. V., of Penance) are taken away or pardoned, according to the more or less perfect disposition of him who receives this sacrament. The third effect is to free him from *venial sins*, and even from *mortal* sins, if there be no possibility of confessing them, or if they have been forgotten, provided there be the repentance of attrition, as we have already shewn in Sect. I. The fourth is *bodily healing*, if it be expedient for the salvation of the soul.

Is there any necessity to receive this Sacrament?

A. You may see clearly, from the importance of the foresaid effects, that every one ought to be careful to fortify himself with this sacrament at the terrible approach of death.

SECT. VII. *Order.*

Is Order a true Sacrament of the new Law?

A. This is an article of the Faith, expressly declared by the Sacred Council of Trent. Order is defined to be;—A Sacrament of the New Law, whereby the spiritual power is given to baptized men, of consecrating bread and wine in the most august Sacrament of the Altar, of administering the Sacraments, and of exercising other ecclesiastical ministries.

What powers must we recognize as derived from this Sacrament?

A. Two powers: the first is called the power of *Order*, which regards the Holy Sacrifice, or the Real Body of Christ; the second is called the power of *Jurisdiction*, which regards the governing of the Mystical Body of Christ, that is to say, of the Christian people.

Have these two powers distinct grades?

A. It is certain that they have distinct grades, of which the Ecclesiastical Hierarchy is formed. It is defined by the Sacred Council of Trent, that there is such an hierarchy. This hierarchy is composed of bishops, priests, and the inferior ministers.

Are several orders to be recognized in Sacred Ordination?

A. It is of Faith that several orders are to be recognized, the Greater Orders and the Minor Orders, as the Sacred Council of Trent has defined.

Which are the Greater Orders?

A. The Greater Orders are three in number: Priest, Deacon, and Sub-deacon.

Which are the Minor Orders?

A. There are four Minor Orders, Ostiarius, Lector, Exorcist, and Acolyte.

Who are the ministers of the Sacrament of Order?

A. Bishops alone, as defined by the Sacred Council of Trent.

What is the *matter* of this Sacrament, and what is its *form* ?

A. The matter is the imposition of the hands of the Bishop upon the person to be ordained ; the form consists of the words with which the Bishop accompanies this action.*

---

* It is to be observed, that in regard to the different greater and lesser Orders, to the Episcopate, and to the matter and form of this Sacrament, much more might be said, but we omit it here, as not necessary for the scope of this work. Moreover, such subjects, being somewhat difficult, would require to be treated at length, in order to be made intelligible to uninstructed persons. [There is required, for instance, in the Western Church, besides the imposition of hands, the tradition of the instruments, that is to say, delivery of the sacred vessels to the person ordained.—ED.]

What dispositions are required in those who aspire to the priesthood ?

A. The principal dispositions are :—1. Vocation from God, for without a positive vocation—which, moreover, must be well examined—no one should dare to aspire to so eminent an estate in the Church. 2. Sanctity of life; for he who does not live habitually in the grace of God, cannot pretend to occupy himself with the most sacred mysteries. 3. The gift of perpetual continence; and he who does not feel himself disposed to preserve this continence should on no account aspire to the sacerdotal state. 4. Competent knowledge; for an ignorant man can never be a useful minister of Holy Church. 5. Immunity from all censures and irregularities.

Cannot the ecclesiastical state be entered on, like any other, when family convenience requires it, provided there be the intention of living in a manner conformable to that state ?

A. No family convenience, nor any other temporal motive, should determine one to embrace that estate, but the Divine vocation alone. He who should receive Holy Orders without such vocation could not expect to live in a manner conformable to the ecclesiastical state, because he could not expect that God would give him the grace which He bestows on those whom He *calls* to serve Him in the priesthood.

Then he who should have received Sacred Orders

without this divine vocation could not hope for salvation ?

A. Such an one would be in great peril ; still, if, considering this peril, and detesting his rashness, he have recourse to the mercy of God, he will obtain the graces necessary for him to save his soul in the state he has entered on, and from which he can never withdraw, because it is a state which is immutable.

What are the *effects* of this Sacrament ?

A. The indelible character which it imprints on the soul, and, 2, grace, as we observed in Sect. I., when speaking of the Sacraments in general.

SECT. VIII. *Matrimony.*

Did Jesus Christ raise the marriage contract to the dignity of a Sacrament?

A. This is an article of the Faith, as affirmed by the Sacred Council of Trent.

Is it lawful for a man to have more than one wife ?

A. Under the Old Law, a man was permitted to have more than one wife at the same time ; but it is forbidden by the New Law. If, however, the first wife dies, it is lawful to take another ; nay, it is an article of the Faith, that to marry successively a second, a third, or a fourth wife is lawful.

Is marriage, after it is consummated, indissoluble?

A. It is an article of the Faith that, in the case of Christians, it is indissoluble. Marriage, in the case of infidels, may be dissolved if the party who is converted to the Faith have good reason for ceasing to cohabit with the party who remains in infidelity.

Is marriage indissoluble when *only ratified*, that is to say, after the marriage has been contracted, but before the wedded persons have yet cohabited?

A. It is an article of the Faith that it may be dissolved by means of religious profession. If the man enters an approved religious Order, and makes his profession, the woman is free; and *vice versa*.

Has the Church authority to declare impediments to marriage, which in certain cases may render the marriage unlawful, and even invalid?

A. This is an article of the Faith, as declared by the Sacred Council of Trent.

Is marriage commanded for all?

A. Marriage is commanded to no one in particular; on the contrary, as of greater perfection, it is better to preserve oneself in perfect chastity. This is also an article of the Faith, recognized as such in all ages of the Church, and so declared by the Council of Trent, where it is defined: "If any one shall say that the married state is to be preferred to the estate of virginity or celibacy, and that it is not a better and a happier condition to remain in virginity or celibacy than to be joined in matrimony, let him be excommunicated."*

* Many other things might be mentioned concerning this Sacrament, but as they are not suited to the primary scope of this little work, it is thought better to omit them.

APPENDIX

ON THE MODE OF TEACHING CHRISTIAN DOCTRINE TO CHILDREN.

SECT. I. *The Importance of this Teaching.*

1. Man's first and highest need is to know God, and the truths which He has revealed. Without this knowledge life must pass unhappily in this world, and will end in eternal misery in the next. This first and highest need of man becomes of urgent necessity, as soon as the light of reason dawns upon the understanding. Hence, while all other kinds of instruction may be deferred till the child has advanced in years, instruction in the truths of religion must not be delayed. On this account the teaching of Christian Doctrine to children is of the highest importance, nay! of absolute necessity.

2. Moreover we must consider that the tenderest age is the best suited for such instruction; for if the first ideas which are communicated to children, when they attain the use of reason, are Christian ideas, these will become, as it were, natural to them, and will remain profoundly impressed on their minds: they will seem to have been born Christians rather than to have been made Christians; nor in later years will they easily suffer those ideas to be altered or effaced. Christian instruction, begun with the first development of the understanding, and carried on afterwards, as it ought to be, with patient and diligent perseverance, is the surest

guarantee we can have that the child will become a good youth and a good man.

3. For this reason, General Councils, the Supreme Pontiffs, and the Bishops have ever prescribed, by most earnest and vigorous precepts, that children should not be left without this instruction; and hence, also, men the most distinguished for learning and sanctity have always promoted it with indefatigable zeal, and have taken delight in making it their own personal care.

SECT. II. *On the Method to be observed in this Instruction.*

1. This instruction should be uniform. Hence children should be taught only the Catechism of the Diocese, and, if possible, made to learn it word for word. Great confusion would be caused by the use of different catechisms. Moreover, a particular form of words is more easily retained, and keeps longer alive in the memory the substance or understanding of the things taught.

2. It is not meant, however, that the mere letter of the catechism is alone to be taught. Persons who are not instructed in theology should confine themselves to this, and content themselves with teaching the catechism as it stands, without expatiating on it or explaining it, because, as they are wanting in the necessary theological knowledge, they might very possibly teach grave error; but let those who are sufficiently instructed endeavour to dilate

upon and explain it according to the children's
capacity, in order that they may the better understand it, and that the truths which it contains may
make a deeper impression on their minds.

3. But be careful not to think it always easy or
desirable to explain too minutely to children the
truths of Christian doctrine.   This is not an easy
matter, because in the mysteries of the Faith we
cannot know all that we should like to know, but
only what God has chosen to manifest to us.   St.
Athanasius said, in regard to the mystery of the Most
Blessed Trinity, that we must be content to know
just so much as the Church teaches us concerning
it, and that the rest is covered by the wings of the
Cherubim.   In like manner, as to the mystery of
the Incarnation, in regard to Grace, and to all
other mysteries, you must not attempt to give a
reason for every difficulty that you meet with, or
expect to understand and be able to explain everything.   Neither is it desirable ; for, even supposing
that he who is teaching Christian doctrine be very
learned, and capable of treating Catholic truths
with profound depth and subtlety, still this would
not be suitable for children, who are scarcely able
to understand the subjects of primary importance,
and that in a general way.   Explain, therefore,
Christian doctrine, but not too minutely, so that
children may learn what is necessary, without having
their minds confused rather than enlightened.

4. Another important caution is, not to touch on

those objections which cannot be answered so as fully to satisfy the unformed intellects of children, nor on those difficulties which cannot be cleared away by evident, or, so to speak, palpable reasons, of which alone the minds of children are capable. Such knowledge as is important for all, should be given to children, and that with the greatest possible clearness and simplicity ; they have not to confute heretics, nor to sit in the chair of the teacher. This caution is very necessary for clerical students, who are sometimes apt to set to work to teach children what they themselves are learning in the schools.

5. Children must be taught *gradually*, beginning with such things as are most necessary to be known, and proceeding from these to the rest ; hence they ought not to be taught a multitude of things at once. For example, you should begin by teaching them the existence of God, His Attributes, the mysteries of the Trinity, the Incarnation, &c., and so lead them on from one subject to another without con-fusion. You must, however, it is true, often recur to the previous subjects, in order that they may not be forgotten. And here I would insist on the im-portance of so explaining the Divine Attributes that children may conceive a *grand idea* of God, and the grandest idea possible ; for this grand idea will be of the utmost service in causing the maxims of the holy Love and Fear of God to make a great impression on their hearts. We know that the reason why God is so little loved and so little feared

by many Christians is, because they have too little knowledge of His Goodness, and of His Greatness.

6. Remember that in teaching children you cannot expect the same success with all. Therefore, let those who are quick and bright, and have good memories, learn more ; while you must be content that those who are slow and dull, and of feeble memory, should learn only those things that are really necessary. You will only lose time if you try to make dull children learn as many things as children of better capacity, and you will only puzzle them. Hence the prudent catechist will seek to instruct children of dull understanding only in such truths as are most important, and indispensably necessary for them to know.

SECT. III. *The Maxims to be instilled into Children.*

1. Teaching children Christian doctrine should not be a bare, dry teaching of the truths of the Faith, such as to tell them : There is a God,—there is a Hell,—there is a Heaven,—there are seven Sacraments, &c.; but it should be a teaching full of life and vigour, which inflames the heart, at the same time that it enlightens the mind. This will be effected by teaching and explaining good Christian maxims ; and I will here put down a few principal ones, by way of example. The first maxim is this ;— that God has placed us in this world, not that we may eat and drink and amuse ourselves, &c., but that we

may know Him, love Him and serve Him now, and afterwards enjoy Him in Heaven; you must thoroughly explain this fundamental maxim, and make children understand, that whoever does not live in this world for the end of knowing, loving and serving God and gaining Heaven, lives ill, and deserves to be removed from the world, just as a vine which does not bear grapes, or a fig tree which bears no figs, would deserve to be cut down and consumed.

2. That the grace of God is the greatest treasure, nay, the only real treasure that there is in the world; that, to preserve the grace of God in our hearts, we should throw overboard the whole world, if it were ours, and if it were necessary so to do in order to preserve the grace of God.

3. That the greatest evil is sin, which deprives us of the grace of God, and that it would be better to keep a live serpent in our bosoms than a mortal sin in our souls; and that, as he who should carry a live serpent in his bosom would be unable to eat or sleep, or amuse himself, from the fear that at any moment this serpent might sting him to death, so it should seem impossible that a person, who has ever so little faith, could eat, or sleep, or amuse himself, while he has on his soul a mortal sin, which at any moment might cast him into Hell; and so, if a child have the misfortune—the greatest of all misfortunes—to commit a mortal sin, he should immediately make a lively act of contrition, and then, as soon as possible, go and confess it.

4. That he who has wicked companions has no need of the devil to tempt him, that he may go to Hell; for it often happens that a wicked companion does more hurt to the soul than the devil himself. Moreover, unrestricted intercourse between boys and girls, if not evil, is always dangerous, and is displeasing to their Guardian Angels.

5. That it is far better not to go to Confession at all, than to make a bad confession by concealing . sins. With this object, it would be well for you to bring forward some terrible example of badly-made confessions.

6. That they must exercise themselves in acts of the love of God, which, according to St Teresa, are like the wood which maintains and increases in the heart the holy fire of God's love. And here it will be well to suggest to children the practice of making them often in the course of the day, such, for instance, as—"My God, I love Thee above all things"—"I love Thee, O Lord, with my whole heart." Theologians are of opinion, that as soon as children attain the use of reason they are bound to make acts of the love of Cod; yet, generally speaking, they are not instructed or incited to fulfil this duty, and, from the natural thoughtlessness of childhood, they themselves think but little of it. In order, therefore, that they may acquire the habit of making frequent acts of the love of God, it will be well for you to examine them from time to time as to this.

7. That a person, truly devout to our Blessed

Lady, was never lost. And here I would exhort you carefully to instil into the hearts of children this tender and fervent devotion, teaching them ever to regard Mary as a most loving Mother, and to have recourse to Her in all their needs. Among other practices you might suggest to them the following easy and most fruitful devotion; that every morning and evening they should say three Aves, adding this short prayer—"Dear Mother, keep me from mortal sin. Dear Mother, let me rather die than offend God."

8. If such and similar maxims are instilled into the hearts of children and young persons, at the same time that you teach them Christian Doctrine, they will be easily trained to goodness and piety : and these maxims, being thoroughly impressed on their hearts in early years, will never be effaced in later life.

SECT. IV. *The qualifications which persons who teach children Christian Doctrine should strive to acquire.*

1. He who has to teach children must be patient, grave, and kind. He must, in the first place, be patient, because children, either from a heaviness of disposition, or from a rude up-bringing, or from thoughtlessness and levity, are often tiresome and difficult to manage. You must compassionate them : all the evil which is in them is not pure malice, and sometimes certain defects

exist which you must put up with. Hence that Saint said well when he said to children: " Be wise, if you can." You must affect not to see many faults and acts of thoughtlessness, which after all are of no great consequence. When the faults are really considerable, you must take the opportunity of scolding them, or punishing them ; but, if a child finds himself scolded and punished for every trifle, while he knows not how to avoid all these scoldings and punishments, he will begin to care for neither the one nor the other, and so will gradually become insensible, and therefore incorrigible.

2. You must preserve a befitting gravity, in order that the children may always have the necessary respect for their master, without which there will be neither attention nor profit. The Catechist, therefore, must always preserve a certain decorum of countenance and manner, in order that the children may respect him. This caution is especially necessary, even on other accounts, for all who teach children.

3. But gravity must not be separated from kindness, in order that children may take pleasure in being with those who teach them Christian Doctrine. If your manners are harsh and repulsive, you will alienate the minds of the children from your teaching, and the few who are present will soon grow weary, be distracted and learn nothing.

4. Those, however, who teach Christian Doctrine with true zeal, will never find themselves deficient

in the requisite qualifications, for the love of God
will teach them how to profit by all means and op-
portunities. Cultivate, therefore, a great love of
God, reflect how important a thing it is to instruct
the mind and form the heart of youth, and then
you may hope for abundant fruit from your labours.
In the eyes of some, those labours may appear
of small esteem and little honour, because they are
expended on children of tender age, and often of
rude natures and low birth, but in the eyes of God,
Who does not regard things with the prejudices of
human vanity, they are of priceless value.

IMPORTANT INSTRUCTIONS REGARDING THE AD-
MINISTRATION OF THE HOLY SACRAMENTS TO THE
SICK.

INSTRUCTION I. *In regard to Confession.*

All Christians, whether men or women, who are
prevented by sickness from repairing to the Church,
even although not in danger of death, may be confessed at home ; and this for many reasons. First,
because they may be in a state of mortal sin, and
so have need of confession that they may regain
the grace of God. Secondly, because it often happens that illnesses, which at the beginning do not
appear dangerous, unexpectedly become serious, so
as even to deprive the patient of the use of his
senses. Moreover, this doctrine goes back to the
Decrees of the Lateran Council under Pope Innocent III. and St. Pius V. These decrees are common both to men and women, as the reasons which
induced the Church to issue them are common to
both. Observe that there is no need to ask the
doctor's permission to receive this sacrament, nay,
that it would be ridiculous to ask the doctor's permission to do that which the Church not only permits but commands.

INSTRUCTION II. *In regard to the Holy Viaticum.*

The Holy Viaticum, according to the teaching of
all Theologians, *may* be administered whenever the

illness is serious, and there is danger of death, although there may yet be good hope of recovery. I say *a serious illness with danger of death*, because a serious illness necessarily implies peril of life; nay, in all grave maladies, fatal and sudden danger is to be feared. Except in clear cases the doctor will judge of the gravity and danger of the illness. But observe, that if the patient have reason to believe his illness serious and dangerous, (provided the doctor do not absolutely affirm the contrary) he may insist on the administration of the Holy Viaticum, even though he may be told, in all sincerity, that his illness is not desperate, nay that there is every probable appearance of his recovery.

INSTRUCTION III. *In regard to Extreme Unction.*

Observe, in the first place, that this Sacrament is so called, not because it is to be administered at the last moment of life, but because it is the extreme, or last of the sacred unctions which the Church gives.

Observe, secondly, that Extreme Unction, like the Holy Viaticum, may be administered every time there is serious illness with danger of death, as already stated. And, as this is a point on which great ignorance commonly prevails, it is well you should hear how St. Alphonsus Liguori speaks of it. Here is a faithful translation of his words : " The Doctors of the Church, such as Suarez, Layman, Castropalao, Bonacina, Conninch, the Salmanticenses and others, are commonly agreed, that it suffices that the sickness be perilous to life, at least *remotely.*" It suffices, therefore, that there be *remote* danger. He goes on to prove this doctrine from the authority of the Councils of Aquisgrana, Magonza, Florence, and Trent. And he then proceeds thus: " This was confirmed still more clearly by Benedict XIV. in the Bull already quoted, in which it is said that the Sacrament of Extreme Unction is not to be administered to those who are in health, but only to those who are seriously ill ; on which ac-count, Castropalao says correctly that whenever the Holy Communion can be given to a sick person as the Viaticum and, therefore, without fasting, Ex-treme Unction may be given, and it is expedient to give it." Therefore, when a sick person has received the Holy Viaticum, he may ask for Ex-treme Unction, and he has a right to receive it.*

These instructions may be useful as rules, not only for the sick themselves, but also for their rela-tions and for doctors.

* At Paris it is customary to give Extreme Unction imme-diately after the Viaticum, as we read in the Life of Victorine de Gallard, who died in 1836. (Life. Part iv.)

PROFESSION OF THE CATHOLIC FAITH.

I, *N. N.*, with a firm faith believe and profess all and every one of those things which are contained in that Creed which the Holy Roman Church maketh use of. To wit:

I believe in One God, the Father Almighty, Maker of heaven and earth, and of all things visible and invisible; and in One Lord Jesus Christ, the Only Begotten Son of God, born of the Father before all ages; God of God; Light of Light; True God of True God; begotten, not made, con-substantial with the Father, by Whom all things were made. Who for us men, and for our salvation, came down from heaven, and was incarnate by the Holy Ghost of the Virgin Mary, and was made man. Crucified also for us under Pontius Pilate, He suffered, and was buried. And the third day He rose again according to the Scriptures; He ascended into heaven, sitteth at the right hand of the Father, and shall come again with glory to judge the living and the dead; of whose kingdom there shall be no end. I believe in the Holy Ghost, the Lord and Lifegiver, who proceedeth from the Father and the Son: who together with the Father and the Son, is adored and glorified; Who spake by the Prophets. And in One, Holy, Catholic, and Apostolic Church. I confess One Baptism for the remission of sins, and I look for

16

the resurrection of the dead, and the life of the world to come. Amen.

I most steadfastly admit and embrace the apostolical and ecclesiastical Traditions, and all other observances and constitutions of the same Church.

I also admit the Holy Scriptures, according to that sense which our holy mother the Church hath held and doth hold, to whom it belongeth to judge of the true sense and interpretation of the Scriptures: neither will I ever take and interpret them otherwise than according to the unanimous consent of the Fathers.

I also profess that there are truly and properly Seven Sacraments of the New Law, instituted by Jesus Christ our Lord, and necessary for the salvation of mankind, though not all for every one: to wit, Baptism, Confirmation, the Eucharist, Penance, Extreme Unction, Order, and Matrimony; and that they confer grace; and that of these, Baptism, Confirmation, and Order cannot be repeated without sacrilege. I also receive and admit the received and approved ceremonies of the Catholic Church, used in the solemn administration of the aforesaid Sacraments.

I embrace and receive all and every one of the things which have been defined and declared in the holy Council of Trent, concerning original sin and justification.

I profess, likewise, that in the Mass there is offered to God a true, proper, and propitiatory sacrifice for the living and the dead. And that in the most holy Sacrament of the Eucharist there is truly, really, and substantially the Body and Blood, together with the Soul and Divinity of our Lord Jesus Christ; and that there is made a conversion of the whole substance of the bread into the Body; and of the whole substance of the wine into the Blood; which conversion the Catholic Church calls Transubstantiation. I also confess that under either kind alone, Christ is received whole and entire, and a true sacrament.

I constantly hold that there is a Purgatory, and that the souls, therein detained, are helped by the suffrages of the faithful.

Likewise, that the Saints, reigning together with Christ, are to be honoured and invocated, and that they offer prayers to God for us, and that their relics are to be had in veneration.

I most firmly assert that the Images of Christ, of the Mother of God, Ever Virgin, and also of other Saints, ought to be had and retained, and that due honour and veneration are to be given them.

I also affirm, that the power of Indulgences was left by Christ in the Church, and that the use of them is most wholesome to Christian people.

I acknowledge the Holy, Catholic, Apostolic, and Roman Church for the Mother and Mistress of all Churches: and I promise true obedience to the Bishop of Rome, Successor of S. Peter, Prince of .the Apostles, and Vicar of Jesus Christ.

I likewise undoubtedly receive and profess all other things delivered, defined, and declared by the Sacred Canons, and General Councils, and particularly by the holy Council of Trent. And I condemn, reject, and anathematize all things contrary thereto, and all heresies which the Church has condemned, rejected, and anathematized.

I, *N. N.*, do at this present freely profess and sincerely hold this true Catholic faith, without which no one can be saved: and I promise most constantly to retain and confess the same, entire and inviolate, by God's assistance, to the end of my life, and to procure, as far as in me lies, that it shall be preached, taught, and observed by all those who depend on me, and all those who shall be committed to my charge.

So help me God.

The Catholic Christian has in this Profession an excellent Act of Faith, and a certain rule by which to recognize all Protestants.

THE END.

R. WASHBOURNE, PRINTER, 18A, PATERNOSTER ROW.

www.ingramcontent.com/pod-product-compliance
Lightning Source LLC
Chambersburg PA
CBHW030644030726
47497CB00006B/1942